THE FOURTH WAY

AND ESOTERIC CHRISTIANITY

By
Rebecca Nottingham

Published by
Theosis Books
© 2009 by Rebecca Nottingham
All rights reserved.
ISBN 0966496035
Printed in the United States of America.

Table of Contents

LECTURE 1   5
AN OVERVIEW OF G.I. GURDJIEFF
AND THE FOURTH WAY

LECTURE 2   41
ESOTERICISM
GURDJIEFF, OUSPENSKY, AND NICOLL
GENERAL DESCRIPTION AND AIM
THE GENERAL STRUCTURE OF THE SYSTEM
LEVELS OF CONSCIOUSNESS
SLEEP
AWAKENING
ESSENCE, REAL I, AND BEING
ACQUIRED (FALSE) PERSONALITY
THE PSYCHOLOGY OF POSSIBLE EVOLUTION

LECTURE 3   69
THE WORK TERMINOLOGY

LECTURE 4   109
THE PRACTICE OF SELF-REMEMBERING
SELF-OBSERVATION
NON-IDENTIFICATION
TEACHERS AND SCHOOLS

LECTURE 1

Early in the Twentieth Century, a Greek-Armenian esoteric teacher walked out of Russia and revolution with a small group of students. His name was George Ivanovitch Gurdjieff. Eventually, he made his way to France and established a teaching center he called the Institute for the Harmonious Development of Man. There, Gurdjieff taught a developmental system on personal transformation that he called The Fourth Way.

In this, what he managed to do was to make metaphysical, spiritual instruction accessible to the rational scientific mind, uniting spiritual teaching from the East with the science of the West. The value of this particular accomplishment is immeasurable. Without Gurdjieff, the practical path of enlightenment called "the Work" may not have reached into the twentieth-century western world. His formulation of this esoteric teaching made it available to the general population where previously it was only found in small exclusive groups few ever heard of.

There is endless gossip about the very enigmatic Mr. Gurdjieff. About his outrageous behavior, about his intentions and moral character, and about his sources. However, there is still much more debate about the system he called The Fourth Way. There seems no end to the constant need to argue or prove the validity of the Fourth Way by way of linking it to esteemed or mysterious sources. More importantly, there seems to be no clear understanding of the subtle, transformational psychological practices of the "Work"—which is the heart and substance of the Teaching. Therefore there are constant questions about how to practice it or why do it at all or what the aim and result is. Gossip and debate will lead you nowhere in your search for meaning and Truth in the Fourth Way. Slander is as easy as idolatry. Only experiential understanding and verification of this Teaching through the practice of it can impart its significance.

Once you have the kind of verification that comes from practice, you cannot misunderstand the aim of it. And once you understand the aim and the Objective Truth found there, you will know how valuable Gurdjieff's contribution was. In the light of it, gossip, personality characteristics and debating the original sources are all irrelevant.

What we have been given in the Fourth Way psychological teaching called the "Work" is a practical, verifiable instruction on the self-development possible for a human being; a process for the real transformation of human consciousness. It teaches self-generated self-transcendence: evolution. It is direction on how to grow in consciousness. By giving you a new perspective and awakened conscience, the Work gives you a chance to choose to become real.

Each of us is born with a nature that springs from the strongest drive in a human being. That drive is self-preservation—the primary survival imperative. The psychological nature produced by this necessary element is based on self-interest and power-seeking is its expression. Human beings naturally strive for power over their environment to help ensure survival and satisfaction. You will find that nearly all that you do can be traced back to one of these elements as motivation. The development possible beyond this automatic self-interested motivation for life is psychological evolution.

Each person's unique essential nature in interaction with its individual environment creates all of the infinite variety of individuals who nevertheless all have the same basic drives creating the same conflicts in lives and events, even in history. This condition would most properly be called humanity's animal level of being. Nearly everyone will live their whole life at that level and die there too, unaware that there is any other way to live. Yet there is much about this level of being that is beneath even animal level behavior, such as killing for pleasure, cruelty, vengeance, sexual perversion, making war, and malice. These things define most people's nature as something below animal nature in character.

A person like this can be said to be in a state similar to being asleep. Governed by self-interest and being automatic in behavior, the person is a stimulus-response organism acting without free will, and is unaware of it. This person spends their life and energy responding mechanically to every changing circumstance, both in external life and in internal states. Each event engenders a response that is subjective and is motivated by gratification-seeking. Constantly changing outside events and internal states create a seamless life of responses one after another. This condition is called Sleep. Everything happens automatically and mechanically.

This is the state of humanity: ASLEEP. From this condition arises every sort of conflict, from resentment to thermo-nuclear annihilation; and every cruelty, every bit of malice, every act of violence. But this is not all what a human being is. In each of us there is also something authentic, with purpose. The Fourth Way calls it "Real I" and teaches that it exists as a possible, that is, reachable state existing within you above the level of the sleeping state of consciousness.

This level is open to the inspiration of Objective Truth which always expresses Goodness because Goodness is above Truth. The direction or inspiration you can receive in this awakened state is from a level above you, from the dimension of Spirit. Therefore, you must raise your own level of consciousness to a place where you can hear higher consciousness—spiritual direction. That means you have to choose, in the moment, to be self-transcendent over all other possibilities.

The possibility of living this way—in the Work—gives meaning to everything in your life. But living it means doing it. It means practicing the exercises and studying the ideas and it means constantly choosing self-transcendent Goodness. One of the most important points to be made concerning "choosing" is that it is an intentional conscious act: you have to make the effort yourself. That effort provides the energy and material for transformation. This is something you can only do by choice, willingly. Choosing Goodness above self-interest creates psychological evolution which happens one person at a time making self-transcendent choices one at a time.

The development or evolution that is possible for a person on this earth in their lifetime is psychological. The result of that self-generated psychological evolution is spiritual growth. Spiritual growth, psychological evolution, higher consciousness, and developed being all mean essentially the same thing: they are describing a higher level within you. All legitimate paths lead in that direction.

From our ordinary state of consciousness we can have very little understanding about how to actually go about becoming a transformed person. Learning to become self-transcendent requires enlightened instruction from someone who possesses an understanding of esoteric teaching. Ouspensky stated, "You must learn from someone who knows". With that instruction, plus knowledge and practical Work, you can create an understanding which raises your level of consciousness. It is your existence in that higher level that manifests your Real I. This can only be a momentary experience at first but it can be built up by conscious intentionality through doing the Work. So there exists real knowledge of how to go about transforming your level of consciousness but it is a painful arithmetical truth that, although the knowledge and the means are available to everyone at all times, few are interested in esotericism and fewer by far find real permanent evolution in the nature of their character—their Being.

Nevertheless, the unconditional love which extends this opportunity to awaken remains faithfully near us, continuously accessible, unchangingly good. Christ's life was lived out in every way necessary to bring all people, under all circumstances, personal communion with God. No other need to, or can, follow Him to the literal cross: it is accomplished. Howsoever anyone finds God, He is the means regardless of what the path is called.

There are legitimate traditional paths to a personal relationship with God; the major religions primarily. They all have esotericism in their essence or in their mystical aspect. However, this teaching about inner development is not expressed very well in external forms, rituals, or dogma. The exoteric forms of all religions very rarely produce real transformation; that is, evolution in the individual. But many ways have always existed in order to accommodate all people.

In Christianity, it is possible to have an authentic transformation by the very simple and completely pure inspiration arising from empathetic experience with Christ and self-transcendent Love for Him. It is possible to be completely changed permanently by sudden radical illumination in the heart and mind which creates objective understanding. It is possible to find transformation through suffering, and although this is God's least desired way, it is a common human path because so many never turn toward God until they are suffering. There is a path to transformation through the selflessly motivated imitation of Christ's nature. There is the salvific way of God-centered life. And because He provided THE WAY, every way eternally, for all, there is also a pathway that is accessible to the intellectual, rational, scientific mind—no particular religious designation required; only conscience. This is esotericism.

The Work is a developmental path for very serious people who cannot find this authentic, permanent change in themselves through academic or inspirational or empathetic or traditional religious means. It is a path of practical psychological instruction intended to purify your heart and mind, resulting in increased consciousness. It is based on Objective Truth and is the essential esoteric teaching given to the world by Christ—the inner meaning of His teaching.

Esoteric doesn't mean 'hidden' or 'secret'. It means 'inner': the inner meaning of a thing. It is uncompromisingly pure; therefore, the steep and narrow path where only the most dedicated will persevere. Since self-transcendence is the elemental force for change at the heart of all real transformation, it is ultimately the only way. Because it is a steep and narrow path, it requires attention and effort. These two supply the energy for change, literally.

The Teaching can be employed by anyone at any time in ordinary daily life. It is an internal, psychological activity and depends entirely on your personal efforts, your motives and a clear understanding of what you are doing and what the aim is. You can supply the first two. Unfortunately, there are few sources that can teach this path correctly or have the right aim. If you are fortunate enough to find such a source, you will be able to verify for yourself the Objective Truth at the heart of the Teaching.

One of the intractable points in the Work is that it is not a passive activity. To listen or read and acquire knowledge is only the initial effort. After that, each person must make personal efforts applying specific practices and exercises that are aimed at enlightenment.

These efforts are almost entirely internal and psychological. The result of these efforts is your authentic selfhood in a state of detachment and purity of heart which is the essential nature of Humility. Doing the Work leads to Humility which requires the greatest courage.

You must understand from the beginning that the Work is a definite process with a specific aim. The Aim of the Work is to develop, that is, raise your level of Consciousness. Your level of Consciousness is correspondingly expressed in your level of Being. Therefore, Being evolves with Consciousness; they are not separable. The ultimate Aim of the process of the Work is to create authentic Goodness in a person; a unified Conscious human being who can act from self-transcendent Goodness instead of self-love.

The process of doing the Work begins with the sincere desire to acquire the Knowledge of ideas and practices. It can only begin to create a transformation within you when you begin to apply the practices and ideas to yourself. Knowing about it, thinking about it, talking about it will not lead to change. Change requires individual internal effort and only the student can supply the force of effort that creates change. In the case of this Work, change means transformation from Sleep to awakened Consciousness, from ego-centric psychology to self-transcendent psychology. The process can be described in general as the purifying of the psychology, which is studied in detail and from a particular angle. This angle is the perspective of uncritical Self-Observation.

Self-Observation is the foundational practice in the Work and it can evolve into a permanent perspective of awareness. Self-Observation is directed at your psychology. It provides illumination for your Work. What you see within yourself in the light of Self-Observation will give you information that you must have for transformation. You cannot reach self-transcendence if you have no self-knowledge. It takes tenacious and repeated efforts to practice Self-Observation correctly; that is, with enough objectivity to be uncritical about what you observe, and enough Conscience to motivate you to change your particular Wrong Work. The illumination from Self-Observation will begin a change within your psychology as you see yourself in the light of Objective Truth.

It is only when you get to this point, after having learned and practiced repeatedly, that you will know what the Work requires of you and you will then have to decide if you want to continue. Every bit of progress depends on your sincere effort, so the continuing is always up to you. If you proceed in the Work you will feel worse before you feel better. You will observe, like a bound-and-gagged prisoner, while your Personality goes around acting in ways and saying things that in no way reflect what is most real in yourself: Real I. You will sound insincere to yourself and you will feel dis-empowered. You will experience a feeling of 'psychological vertigo' as you lose Acquired Personality before True Personality has had time to grow. But you will come to a point, intermittently at first, when the strength of Real I can direct Personality. Your Work Memory, which is the memory of everything that you have verified for yourself through your practice, will grow and gain clarity and have force.

You will find that this process of gaining something—Consciousness—requires mostly losing things, like the ordinary thoughts and emotions that make up the noise in your mind, so that there is a place inside that can hear. You will find that you have to Work your way up, through intentional effort, to a place where you can begin to receive illumination from Higher Consciousness. And what you will find is that the psychological position from which you can be receptive is characterized by Humility. Humility has no requirements and thereby enough inner silence to hear.

Be sure that this is what you are seeking—To be humble and pure in heart and at the service of Goodness. If you are seeking personal power in worldly terms you will not find it in the Work. Don't come to the Work expecting to be gifted with great transforming experiences. You will receive tools. You will have to use them yourself to create transformation out of effort—WORK. You will experience resistance internally and externally. You will no longer be going with the flow. You will have turned around and so the flow will be going against you.

There are many books by and about Gurdjieff and his students and the Fourth Way. For this reason, I would prefer not to dwell on material that can easily be found elsewhere. Also, what can be assumed about the Work of the Fourth Way from a position outside of it, has little to do with the incandescent reality of it, making historical and anecdotal material irrelevant.

What I want to address here are some specific problems present in the current generation of teaching the Work. The Work is the psychological methodology of the Fourth Way. There are numerous ways in which it has been distorted, making the real essence of it inaccessible. That loss has caused many to lose their souls to the corruption of this spiritual path into the business of buying and selling self-empowerment.

Regarding the current generation of Fourth Way groups, some forms represent the perversions or distortions or level of Being of their various leaders unintentionally. Some forms remain rigidly crystallized in formatory dogma and structure to assure absolute adherence to Gurdjieff's literal words and idolization of his person. Some forms have been created that deliberately misuse the ideas and misrepresent the Teaching for the purpose of personal gain for the teacher.

While the distortion of the idea of "esoteric" into a secret society mentality held some validity in the world at the beginning of the twentieth century, it remains a distortion, nonetheless, in the Work of the Fourth Way. It is still employed as a selling tactic because people love secrets. They love being told secrets. They love keeping secrets and they love telling secrets. They love the superiority and power they feel when they know something that another does not. When something is secret, it appears to be special and those who have access to it feel special themselves. Selling secrets always works because the buyer feels empowered.

But in the Work, esoteric means 'inner'—the inner meaning of a thing. It does not mean 'hidden' or 'secret'. In the case of the Work, it literally is the inner meaning of Christ's Teaching on personal transformation—spiritual development. Gurdjieff called it "Esoteric Christianity" as did his primary students Ouspensky and Nicoll. Esoteric teaching is not hidden.

It would be nearly impossible to conceptualize the Fourth Way teaching from Gurdjieff's writings alone. Ouspensky expressed it in the intellectual terms of a cosmological system, a new model of the universe based on esoteric teaching. Nicoll's contribution is of no less consequence as he aligns it with the Objective Truth expressed most clearly in esoteric Christianity. Not one of these men was a perfected human being. They each had their respective subjectivity to deal with, yet they each accomplished something extraordinary. Together they left enlightened instruction about self-generated evolution: the Work. It is a sacred Path.

Today's age of global mass media and computer technology has put an end to esoteric secretness. Virtually all available knowledge is accessible to anyone interested. Unfortunately, what seekers will find in the representative Fourth Way Schools or groups is a degenerated version taught without the intended context or aim. The "secret society" ideology of elitism is perpetuated, as well as teacher worship and legalism, in lieu of substantive instruction and directed process. Meaning has become about gaining personal power and gratification rather than self-transcendence and increasing consciousness.

The Work is a path to a level where your consciousness shares communion with God through the conduit of Spirit. In misrepresenting this Aim, the Fourth Way System can be and has been manipulated to entrap students and bilk them and cause harm to their psychology. It is meant to heal and purify your psychology and enlighten your Consciousness. It is being used against vulnerable students to rape their souls and their bank accounts. As in conventional exoteric religion, people hear the resonance of Truth and they are attracted to it. However, they do not find Truth in the Gurdjieff schools or groups. What can be found are cults of varying success. Potential students are misled and used and prevented from developing in the Work by the very teachers and organizations supposedly teaching them the Fourth Way.

It has been made easy to employ this kind of corruption not only because of the omission of context and aim, but also because Gurdjieff taught a specific cosmology, including manners of expression, that can captivate and fascinate endlessly. Or these same expressions can lead a student into the psychological, transformational ideas of the Work. The Work is not the Cosmology and it is not 'the Movements', though they have a place in the system. The Work is the psychological Teaching at the heart of the Fourth Way. It is the inner meaning of the Fourth Way. It is the esoteric meaning behind the Cosmology and the Movements. All aspects of the cosmology cannot be verified literally and 'the Movements' are clearly not possible for every student seeking transcendence. The Work, which is accessible and verifiable to all, is the only aspect of the Fourth Way that can create psychological transformation in the student. It is ONLY the psychological part of the Teaching, the Work, that contains the means for transformation.

The Work is fundamentally different from other paths to conscious development in a few very important ways. To begin with, although it is a psychological system, the Work differs from standard psychology's presuppostion that a human being has consciousness. Modern psychology presumes that a person who is awake and walking around has consciousness. The Work asserts that every person in this waking state is in reality in a state of Waking Sleep, and that there is very little consciousness present. But it also teaches that consciousness can be developed through specific intentional efforts. The Work teaches how to develop your consciousness through ideas and psychological practices that build a new kind of understanding. It requires a great inner struggle against the assertions of Personality and against the momentum of being Asleep in life.

The next idea is one that is essential in the direction of the Work. It differs from every religious tradition and humanity's general presupposition that God's will is done on earth. God's will is not done on earth and this is verifiable. All of the evil and suffering that you see in the world are not the results of God's will, for God's nature is ONE. That one characteristic is Perfect Goodness. It is the will of individuals acting and living out of self-interested motivations that creates the chaos of violence and suffering. The will of God is not done on earth. The will of man is done on earth. If you believe that God's nature is something other than perfect Goodness, what are you worshipping? Only Goodness is worthy of worship.

Nicoll:

". . . Religious people usually imagine that what happens on earth is always God's will, and they seek to comfort and strengthen one another with this thought, even in the face of the most senseless and fortuitous accidents, disaster and death. People who are not religious take it as evidence that there is no God. . . . People judge of the existence or non-existence of God from what happens on earth. Every decade books are written proving that the existence of God is impossible in view of the fact that there is so much evil in life, and so much cruelty and waste in nature, while most people in the privacy of their own thoughts come to a similar conclusion. In the face of this, and arguing from the standpoint of the visible world, is it possible to believe that God—as the supreme principle of highest Good—exists? . . . If we always look to visible life for evidence of the existence or non-existence of God nothing will come of it. Therefore, to draw conclusions about God from what happens on earth is to start from an entirely wrong point of view. People continually start from this wrong level. . . . They regard the visible external world as the first theater of divine vengeance and see in its events the hand of God punishing or rewarding human beings according to their behavior. They see God as right or justice on earth. They see the hand of God in war and believe that God is on their side and that victory will mean that the will of God is fulfilled. It is this external, sense-based idea of religion that is rebuked by Christ. He says that all people suffer the same fate unless they repent, but what is to *repent*?

The word translated throughout the New Testament as repentance is in the Greek *metanoia* which means change of mind. The Greek particle meta is found in several words of comparatively ordinary usage, such as metaphor, metaphysics, metamorphosis. Let us take metaphor; it means transference of meaning. To speak metaphorically is to speak beyond the literal words, to carry over or beyond and so transfer the meaning of what is said beyond the words used. Metaphysics, again, refers to the study of what is beyond purely observable physical science, such as the study of the nature of Being or the theory of knowledge or the fact of consciousness. Metamorphosis is used to describe the transformation of form in insect life, the transformation of a grub into a butterfly—a transference or transformation of structure into an entirely new structure, into something beyond. The particle meta therefore indicates transference, or transformation, or beyondness. The other part of this word translated as repentance—noia—is from the Greek words nous which means mind. The word metanoia has to do with the transformation of the mind in its essential meaning.

Nicoll:

"Here lies one of the deepest ideas in the psychological teachings of the Gospels. A radical, permanent transformation is taught as being possible and Metanoia is the technical description of it. But a man cannot reach a permanent higher level of himself unless there is built up in him a connection of ideas that can gradually lift him beyond his present level. The idea of the self-evolution of Man, the idea of Metanoia or transformation of mind, and the idea of the Kingdom of Heaven are all connected and related ideas. . . . Christ's teaching is about a possible individual evolution in a man. . . . Everyone on this planet is capable of a certain inner growth and individual development, and this is his true significance and his deepest meaning, and begins with Metanoia."

The Work is a Teaching about the process called Metanoia which is a psychological transfiguration.

There is an important common element in most religious teachings, ancient ones as well as New Age metaphysical ideologies and many popular belief or developmental systems, that is inconsistent with Objective Truth. It is also another way that the Work is very different from other paths. Almost all popular developmental systems teach that spiritual growth—developed Consciousness—results in material world gains, especially wealth and health. The ideology maintains that higher consciousness or psychological/spiritual growth heals the physical body and provides wealth in the physical world. This is not correct. The material world cannot determine development in the spiritual or metaphysical realm. Nor can metaphysical gain be counted or seen in earthly materiality. What is possible, and has been distorted, is that by raising your level of Being you will attract different influences and different circumstances because your Being attracts your life.

Anything can happen to your body and eventually everyone's body suffers and everyone's body dies. You need not allow your psychological state to depend upon your material world circumstances. You can develop Consciousness and Being regardless of your physical condition or any circumstances. Since the developmental path is essentially always above you, available to you in each moment, your condition in life is not a limitation to your possible level of Consciousness. This is a spiritual Truth and it is easily verifiable. One clear objective observation will verify for you that health and wealth have nothing to do with a person's spiritual nature or level of Consciousness. The most successful and active people in the world are hardly correspondingly deeply spiritual or developed in Consciousness or Being. Nor are the most authentically developed and spiritual people necessarily among the wealthy, jogging elite.

These ideas are misinterpreted even within legitimate traditional systems. They are a lower level of understanding, expressing a spiritual truth, and deliberately or not, they sell well. It is mixing different levels of Understanding. It is attributing to spiritual growth a corresponding material growth. It is saying that your worldly life will become perfect if your spiritual life becomes perfect. This is wishful thinking at best. Witness the lives of the saints. Anything can happen to anyone in life, including poverty and illness. But nothing can happen in life to anyone that can inhibit the development of Consciousness. Developed Being, which is the expression of Consciousness, can accept life as it is, and continue to express and create and live in Goodness.

That is not to say that your psychology or spiritual disposition has no effect on your physical body, but it is a serious mistake to believe that any particular path will result in perfect life in the physical world because: if physical world gain is any part of your motivation for being on a spiritual path, you will develop nothing. The angle of approach is wrong and not accessible to the level of spirit. It makes your efforts conditional and self-interested, which is antithetical to transcendence.

This great lie—that followers of any particular teaching will have earthly superiority and powers including health and wealth—seduces people away from the possibility of real spiritual transformation since real spiritual transformation is dependent upon the purity of your motives and means moving from egocentric psychology to self-transcendent psychology: evolution.

From the self-transcendent stage you will see the partial truth which creates these mis-formulations. You will understand that a higher level of Consciousness and spiritual growth are the same thing. And that from a higher level of Consciousness—spiritual understanding—the concerns and interests you have in life change and your detachment from the circumstances of your life leave you content with what is. You are not as interested in what you can get or do, as in what you can give and become.

Real developed Being has patience and peace. It is content to wait or to act without requirements because living in Being is rich with meaning. Whether external life is difficult or easy remains irrelevant because your heart and mind are walking in the right path. That gives meaning to every day and the opportunity in every moment to be on the path; in this case, to be in the Work.

There is another very important practice that is constantly misused especially in Fourth Way schools. It is the practice of bringing your awareness into the present moment. If this psychological exercise is used correctly, it is a tool. Practicing correctly means precisely "bring your awareness into the present moment". This exercise will remove you from the mechanical momentum of life and your Identification with it. Instead of being totally Asleep and caught up in automatic responses, you raise your awareness from that hypnotic state into cognizance of the present moment you are living. First, by sensing your body in the here and now and then by expanding your awareness to include your body in its surroundings, and from your immediate environment to a broader scale. You notice that you feel tense, that your brow is furrowed or you are tapping your foot or your stomach is clenched and you intentionally release the energy and relax. You deny any thoughts or emotions access to your attention which is focused in the moment. You look, you register, you release tension and you are not part of the mechanical stream of life for a few moments. You may feel a stronger sense of Real I as a result.

This is a very minor form of practicing Self-Remembering by stepping out of your mechanical awareness for a moment. It is a valuable exercise that can take you out of the momentum of Sleep, give you an experience of scale and some awareness of Self outside of that mechanical momentum. It also gives the practitioner an experience of relief from identification and negative emotions "in the moment". It is this last part that has been perverted in Fourth Way instruction where this exercise is called Self-Remembering, which it is not, and where the student is taught to meet every difficulty with Self-Remembering. If the student could practice full Self-Remembering, then they would be working rightly. But Self-Remembering has many forms and degrees. The beginning student cannot jump up into the presence of Real I, because Real I is yet unknown and unformed so there is no place in which to jump.

If you observe carefully you will see that the expansion of consciousness is horizontal, on the level of life in the world. It starts with becoming aware of yourself physically and expands to being aware of yourself contextually, physically. While this exercise can provide valuable knowledge, it is a tool, not an end. It is not the road to Conscious Evolution. It is one of many tools used to create a certain kind of awareness and in that, it is helpful. It does not create Real I, it clears the way for sensing it momentarily, and most importantly it is not Self-Remembering.

The misuse of this practice in the Fourth Way happens when a student gets addicted to the feeling of relief from Identification or painful emotions, even for a few moments, then it is a tool used for emotional disassociation. Or, when the student is taught to use this practice to become Non-Identified whenever they experience Negative Emotions. Used in this way, it becomes an escape mechanism and does not allow the student the chance to Observe and recognize and separate from the Wrong Work that keeps creating the Negative Emotions.

The student stays trapped in a blind alley when the experience of Negative Emotions is treated with this exercise; i.e. Negative Emotions = bring awareness into the physical world experience of now = temporary emotional relief = no clear Observation of what the Negative Emotion is and what it is connected to in the psychology = no means to deal with it or understand it or Work against it to create transformation. So the student practicing wrongly cannot build a structure of Understanding that would eventually raise them to a permanent level of Non-Identification. They can only try to jump up and touch that state over and over again. Touching that state is possible. Living in it requires building it. Building it requires long term attention and effort.

The Work gives us many tools and ideas with which to create transformation. The primary most essential exercise given is Self-Observation. It is through Self-Observation that you learn to see your own psychology functioning. You learn to "Know Thyself" through Self-Observation. It is the fundamental practice from which all development grows. In comparison, the exercise of "being present" provides little knowledge with which to Work.

So this distorted practice stops the developmental process and prevents the student from gaining the understanding received through Self-Observation. It also keeps the student enslaved to the "school" since development can't come from this wrong way of practicing.

Another distortion which is taught in Fourth Way schools appeals to the desire to avoid suffering each person experiences. The claim is made that the Work teaches you how to stop suffering. The truth of the Teaching is that you learn to stop unnecessary suffering which is not the same thing. Sacrificing your suffering, learning how to become objective to it, detached from it, is not anything like emotional disassociation which is the result of wrong practicing. Emotional disassociation is the wrong work of the Emotional Center and completely limits your ability to receive the Work. Through the active process of the Work you will learn what Unnecessary Suffering is and become free of it. But the idea is sold that higher consciousness is free of human suffering. This is not true. In some ways it suffers less, in some ways it suffers more. The idea of Non-Identification is clarity and purity in the Emotional Center, not separation from it.

There is another very heavy-handed misrepresentation of an esoteric idea taught in most successful Fourth Way schools. The idea is that of "payment" and the distortion is again assigning literal meaning to a psychological truth. The Gurdjieff "schools" teach that you have to pay for what you receive, specifically in money and services, to the school. The principle is supposed to be that if you pay money for it, you will value it more and the idea is used to convince students that they have to give enormous amounts of money to the "school": dues, special donations, fines, etc., in order to receive the Teaching. It goes without saying that schools have financial needs and it is appropriate that the students who are able to share that burden do so. But this is not the esoteric idea of payment.

The idea that you have to pay for what you receive is accurate when understood psychologically. The Truth of this spiritual principle is that in order to gain in Consciousness or Being, i.e. evolve, you must sacrifice something. The reason behind it is that you must give up something internally in order to make room for the developing Consciousness. If you cling to the mechanical conditions that keep consciousness asleep and you give up nothing, then change is impossible. Without sacrifice there is no space internally for growth and change. Change is essential. You cannot change and remain the same. In the Work, change means sacrificing self-interest. That sacrifice is your payment, spiritually/psychologically speaking.

Consequently, there is Objective Truth in the idea that each person must make a "payment" in order to receive from the Teaching. The psychological Truth in the Work is that your "payment" is the effort you make, each effort you make, to awaken. When, for instance, you have sacrificed your need to be right, what you receive is the freedom from the psychological tyranny and suffering of always having to be right. This is the correct Work understanding of payment and receipt. The whole concept of sacrifice in the Work must be understood correctly or no development is possible.

In almost every teaching, this idea is used to squeeze volunteerism and cash out of the student. You are taught that you must sacrifice your time and energy to contribute to the community through manual labor or services and of course you must contribute money, whether or not you can afford it. Without saying that these kinds of sacrifices have no potential value, it is critical to understand that what the Work asks you to sacrifice is your suffering; that is, your Unnecessary Suffering. Self-Observation will illuminate for you everything that you have to sacrifice, and differentiate between Unnecessary Suffering and Necessary Suffering. Self-Observation with Work knowledge and Conscience will reveal to you everything that you must sacrifice in order to develop Consciousness.

The whole idea of sacrifice has been so polluted with perversions that it is a vital concern that you understand that in the Work you make sacrifices by making the effort to apply the ideas to yourself. That effort may include gaining knowledge, opening your mind, directed thinking, intentional use of your attention and energy, sincerity, honesty, dedication, and actually practicing the psychological exercises of Self-Observation, Inner Separation, Non-identification, External Considering, and much more. These ideas are so dense that it is only through the experiential Verification of the practices that you can understand what they mean. Then you will begin to understand what you need to sacrifice and how you can sacrifice. The first thing that you will understand is that this sacrificing is a psychological/spiritual exercise, not a material-world directive.

If you take this idea of sacrifice externally, that is exoterically, it is simple math to see how the axiom becomes: "the bigger the sacrifice, the bigger the gain". This level of understanding renders every perversion from poor people sending their life savings to televangelists, to intentionally creating suffering in order to generate a bigger sacrifice, and even to the literal sacrifice of human life. The sacrifice of every external thing is always easier (the path of least resistance) than the sacrifice of ego, of Acquired Personality, of Pictures you have of yourself, of Inner Considering and all sorts of Identification. It is easier and it is dangerous. Beware of religions, schools, developmental paths or systems that ask you to sacrifice your money and your time in payment to them. They have either misunderstood something fundamental about real Conscious development or they are knowingly misusing this idea for their own gain. If you Work right and sacrifice right and have actual psychological transformation, then you will want to give back to what has given this miracle to you. At this point inspiration will let you know how to give back and the means will be different for everyone. Volunteerism and even money then become gifts of gratitude and appreciation, not payment. Gifts are pure.

Another of the central ideas of the Gurdjieff teaching that has been mis-taught is the idea of building a soul. This is a very foundational idea and is a misunderstanding of the spiritual concept intended or perhaps simply a miscommunication of the process. In the Fourth Way cosmology it is taught that you can build a soul that exists in Eternity (in the electronic world, so to speak) through conscious efforts. The spiritual reality is that everything that does not come from higher consciousness passes into nothing because it issues from sleep. Sleep cannot produce something eternal. Therefore, you cannot build your own soul since you do not possess higher consciousness. You can build your consciousness which can result in the actualization of your soul. However, what you find in higher consciousness is that you receive your soul rather than build it. Developing higher consciousness is soul-saving; salvific life. And it is sacrifice that creates the internal space which receives it.

The esoteric teaching is that you must organize your three given bodies in order to have access to your divine body. This is "building" only in the sense of creating the conditions necessary to possess the fourth divine body. What the possession of divine body means regarding the life of the soul is unknowable. It certainly does not mean that you as you are now can have immortality in divine light. It means whatever good you do becomes a conduit of light and is continued in the realm of divine light and therefore immortal. The idea of possessing your own personality eternally, through immortality, ought to frighten you into getting very serious.

Since this Teaching is esoteric Christianity, the real understanding of this idea is not that you have to build your soul because if you could create it yourself the result would be a sort of Frankenstein made from the distortions of your own limitations. What you can do, through the Work, is to create a purified place within yourself where what is called the Holy Spirit in traditional Christian terms can exist within you. This place is in Higher

Consciousness. Higher Consciousness, being on a completely different level, has a different psychological orientation than Sleep. If there is no place within you that is clean enough of self-interest, then you are not accessible to higher influences and the Spirit cannot penetrate and baptize you because there is no receptive place where it can enter.

The Work is about purifying your psychology and emotions, cleaning a place within in order to be open, to be able to be receptive and hear from what the Work calls higher influences—or from Higher Consciousness, or from what is above, spiritually speaking.

So the process of baptism in the Esoteric Christian tradition is the opposite of the exoteric ritual of submerging an individual in water. To symbolically immerse the individual in the Holy Spirit is a reversal of the real process. It is not you who enters the Holy Spirit and comes out imbued with it. The Holy Spirit enters you, and only to the extent that you have a place that is receptive within. The Work makes this place. The experience is universal, therefore the process and transformational experience is the same for all people in all times. Since it is recognizable in different forms, it is verifiable.

If you are interested in the powers you will gain through doing the Work you should know exactly what they are. You will be able to transcend your personal desires on behalf of the greater good. You will no longer feel competitive. You will not feel the need to assert yourself, but you will be able to, if appropriate. You will feel comfortable within yourself. Your actions will be motivated by Goodness only, because Goodness is the nature of developed Being. Your Real I will not be tossed around by the circumstances of life. Real I will simply respond appropriately, always creating Goodness. You will suffer less, subjectively, and you will suffer more, objectively. Your Conscience will grow and assert influence that can create real permanent change—evolution. You will experience peace, acceptance, serenity, appreciation, gratitude, joy, humility, forgiveness, freedom, conscious inspiration, intentionality in action.

You may well have heard some of these ideas from other sources in devolved forms. The potential powers offered to the student in existing Fourth Way schools are from the psychological level of sense-based thinking. They appeal to Personality. They say you will gain self-mastery and the power to "do". You will awaken to the illusion of life. You will become a higher self, an improved version of yourself. You will discover your Real I. You will become free of the ordinary laws that govern other people's lives and be able to act intentionally and get the results you desire. You will receive hidden knowledge not available outside of the "school". You will learn how to experience higher conscious states. You will come under the direct power of C Influence. You will have understanding that sleeping humanity does not possess. You will learn esoteric secrets about how to create your soul.

You will be able to create your own soul and that will give you immortality.

It is important to note that none of these expressions of powers are a complete lie. They are a lower level expression of the Objective Truth behind them, consequently, a distortion. They do not express the context or the aim of the Work. They are aimed at attracting Personality. Whether that distortion is intentional or a manifestation of a lack of Being isn't really the point. The point is that a person cannot grow in the Work if their motives are self-interested. Self-interested motives cannot be served by the Work because Higher Consciousness depends on self-transcendence.

Therefore everyone coming into the Work needs to understand from the outset that it is far more about giving up self-interest and giving up gratification-seeking, than gaining personal worldly power and self-mastery in the ordinary sense. Also that this giving up of self requires immeasurable efforts—WORK.

All of the Work is to raise your level of Consciousness and evolve your level of Being. It is personal, interior, psychological Work because that is where development can happen. Your Being, which is a manifestation of your Consciousness, is also an expression of your psychology. The aim of the process is to deconstruct the Acquired Personality by way of efforts that illuminate and disempower it. The objective here is to purify the psychology of what is false and inauthentic and self-interested and negative because these psychological conditions obstruct the development of Consciousness. These elements are studied, addressed, and transcended leaving a more purified heart and mind, feelings and thoughts; i.e. psychology.

This Work, which begins with self-knowledge, is called self-evolution because it is only through sincere efforts intentionally made by yourself, that the possibility of evolution exists. It is in and through the energy of the effort that evolution happens. Each person must make their own efforts—Work—in order to evolve. No one can evolve by intellectual understanding, by vicinity, by osmosis, or by knowledge. Only personal Work effort produces the force for evolution.

In the Fourth Way, the Work ideas belonging to this esoteric teaching are about personal, psychological evolution and they require real personal efforts to create experiential Understanding. You may take the Gurdjieffian cosmology or leave it, but no one can advance in the Work, gain in evolution of Consciousness and Being, without practicing and applying the psycho-transformational ideas to themselves with sincerity and tenacity. If the ideas are understood rightly and practiced in earnest, the results are the development of Consciousness and Being.

By selling the Work as a system to develop personal power and even immortality, many are attracted; especially those who have already dangerously formed egos. Most are easily satisfied by paying money to receive supposedly secret knowledge that will transform them automatically and bestow the aforementioned powers. Ironically, the kind and degree of vanity which falls for this angle of approach to the Work hasn't a chance to grow past its self-interest, which is the Aim of the Work. Their motives defeat them from the outset. It is not an easy process, it is life-long, and it is for people who are very serious about becoming authentic and good and who long for change enough to be able to accomplish it.

Not many people will even discover and fewer will choose a serious path of permanent transformation. Perhaps the reason is no more complicated than the fact that the path of least resistance holds the most power of attraction for mechanical humanity.

Christ's suffering in life and death were not the will of God. In part it was a sacrifice demanded by the character of human nature in order to impart an exemplary experience that can be grasped by anyone, anytime. His suffering and death were a necessary dimension of his earthly life intentionally undertaken so that communion with the whole of humanity through divine love was made possible. This was an, unfortunately, necessary sacrifice, willingly given by God in Christ. Given in love to teach us to know God and how to love one another.

Contextualizing a path of conscious development based in sound Christology is an advantage since there exists a valid, verifiable teaching and a Divine Teacher. But the psychological Work of self-transformation belongs to a methodology that is unilaterally accessible to all, regardless of religious or secular designation. Having a religious longing is definitely an advantage, but this indescribable yearning is called by many names in the world and most find themselves confused about what they are seeking. Then they are easily satisfied to find any emotional experience of a religious nature sufficient to their needs. But for those few who are diligent in their search for authentic meaning, some fortunate ones will find the path of esoteric Christianity called the Work.

Objective Truth is the highest level of Truth. It is unchanging throughout time and under every circumstance. Like water, it moves to accommodate life while staying the same substance: Objective Truth. It is verifiable through experiential Understanding. The process and result of verification is an individual, internal event yet also the same for everyone in every time period.

Christ's life was a sacrificial model to meet the needs of the level of development of humanity. Its multi-dimensional nature makes it accessible to all, always. But he gave a teaching as well—an authentic methodology which is instruction on spiritual development. In the Work this instruction is formulated into psychological practices with the aim of developing a higher level of Consciousness. It is instruction on how to become a person Holy in Being and in life; this life now; your life while you are here and can be of service. What happens after this life is unverifiable. You have to do the Work for the love of it, from the Valuation you have for the gift it is to your life, from the gratitude you feel for being given meaning and a way to walk in Goodness toward your highest Self.

LECTURE 2

These lectures are intended to give you an understanding of the Fourth Way System which is an esoteric teaching about the inner development possible for human beings. You will learn about the relationship between Christian esotericism and the Fourth Way. You will hear instruction about the ideas, the practices and exercises, the terminology, the process and aim, the requirements and result of becoming a student of the Fourth Way. At the end of these lectures, you should clearly know what the Fourth Way is and whether it is the path you wish to follow.

Esoteric teaching is a psychological system but it differs from today's version of psychology. Modern scientific psychology studies Man as it finds him or as it supposes him to be. The psychology of esotericism studies Man from the point of view of his possible evolution. This perspective on psychology is the one being used in these talks -- the point of view of Mans possible evolution.

* * * *

ESOTERICISM

Esotericism is all teaching regarding the inner development of Man. Esoteric teaching is a special kind of knowledge that has to be learned and gradually understood through emotional development. It is intended to produce a profound and authentic permanent change in the individual.

Esoteric teaching has existed throughout human history in different forms and schools. At different periods, it has been sown into the world to give us direction. Nicoll: In every age, there is sown into the world esoteric teaching which gives the direction in which individual evolution should take place....In our epoch, we have been given the esoteric teaching in the gospels indicating the direction in which individual evolution should take place at this stage.

The word esoteric is commonly misunderstood to mean secret or hidden. Esoteric schools have existed for many thousands of years, but in the pre-industrial-technological world they consisted of relatively small isolated groups. The vast majority of humanity never heard of esotericism and extremely few people came into contact with a real school. The secret society mentality about esotericism arose partly from this ignorance due to circumstances and it is used in current Fourth Way schools as a selling tactic. People love secrets, they love elitism, hats, and agreed-upon delineated hierarchical groups. But esoteric does not mean secret or hidden, it refers to the inner meaning of a thing. Gurdjieff: In the first place, this knowledge is not concealed; and in the second place it cannot, from its very nature, become common property. Esoteric knowledge is not hidden, it is available, however, the enormous majority of people cannot hear it or if they do, they find it fantastic, or at least unnecessary.

Esoteric teaching is for those who are not satisfied with themselves or with life as it is, those who feel there must be some greater meaning to life and yearn to find their own meaning in it. If you are mostly satisfied with yourself, with the kind of person you are, esotericism is not the path for you. You must have a question in yourself and feel a longing for understanding, for completeness and personal meaning and direction. Then, if you seek, when you find you will be able to hear.

GURDJIEFF, OUSPENSKY, AND NICOLL

Gurdjieff (1872-1949)
So much has been written about the very enigmatic George Ivanovitch Gurdjieff that anyone would be hard pressed to sort out fact from fiction or in this case, slander from idolatry. Gossip is easy and second-hand information is subjective. What is commonly accepted is that he was Greek-Armenian, trained from his childhood in the Sufi tradition and he was possibly an Orthodox

monk at some point. Also, he traveled extensively through Egypt, Greece, India, and the Caucasus seeking out schools of esotericism. In 1917, he left Russia with a small group of students and eventually settled in France in 1922. There he purchased a residence at Fontainebleau and opened what he called the Institute for the Harmonious Development of Man where he taught the Fourth Way.

His methods were controversial and his personal behavior sometimes outrageous. There has always been debate about his motives, his actions, and his legitimacy. Mr. Gurdjieff can only be encountered in the Fourth Way Work, in the System he taught. In the light of understanding the Work, its magnitude and significance, you encounter Gurdjieff and thereafter gossip or arguing about his sources becomes irrelevant. The beauty and importance of the Fourth Way which he introduced to western civilization validates his authenticity, but in spite of his reputation and accomplishment and flamboyant personality, he remained humble. He gave this very stern warning to potential students: Never confuse the vessel with the cargo.

Ouspensky (1878-1947)
Peter Demianovich Ouspensky was born in Moscow. He was an intellectual and a journalist for some years and traveled in the east and Europe and Russia. In 1907, he

discovered the idea of esotericism and pursued the study of it in many different countries and methods. His search took him to Egypt, Greece, India, Ceylon and many other countries. He also studied occult literature, yogis, Tarot, and magical methods. He gave public lectures on his search for the miraculous.

He met Gurdjieff in 1915 in Moscow and was so impressed that he arranged groups to whom Gurdjieff presented his teaching. Ouspensky and Gurdjieff had a rocky personal relationship. In 1918, Ouspensky began to feel that I had ceased to understand him and found it necessary to separate Gurdjieff and the system, of which I had no doubts. In 1922 he helped Gurdjieff move to Fontainebleau in France and subsequently visited there several times. Ouspensky finally broke acrimoniously with Gurdjieff in 1924 but continued his work in London. After his death in 1947, the manuscript of his book Fragments of an Unknown Teaching was sent to Gurdjieff who said: Before I hate that man, now I love that man. The book was published in 1949 and retitled In Search of the Miraculous.

Nicoll (1884-1953)
Maurice Nicoll was born in Kelso, Scotland into a titled family. He attended college and qualified as a physician and eventually became a practicing psychologist in London. He spent several years studying in Paris, Berlin and Vienna, and worked with Carl Jung for some time. In 1914, he served with the R.A.M.C. in Gallipoli and Mes-

opotamia during World War I. Upon returning to England, he was a medical officer in charge of the Empire Hospital which treated men with head and spinal injuries.

He met Ouspensky in 1921 and became interested in the Teaching. Some time later he closed his practice in London and went to live at the Institute at Fontainebleau where he worked with Gurdjieff directly. When he returned to England, he received Ouspensky's permission to pass on the ideas he had received from both teachers. He began teaching in 1931 in England and continued until his death in 1953.

GENERAL DESCRIPTION AND AIM

The Fourth Way is an esoteric teaching about the personal development of consciousness possible for a human being. Man is created as a self-evolving being. Nicoll: Man is sown on earth...with the possibility of inner development, and the existence of this Work, the existence of Christ's teaching and the existence of many other teachings, is due solely to this fact -- that Man is created as an organism capable of undergoing an inner evolution.

This system uses ideas, practices, and exercises designed to bring about a gradual change in the level of your understanding, in the perspective of your mind and in the nature of your character. It can be practiced in life -- your life, as it is now. There is no need to remove yourself from your circumstances and go into a separate community in order to be in the Fourth Way. Its psychological methodology is meant to be practiced in your daily life with all of the circumstances and people belonging to it.

It requires two kinds of effort -- work on your knowledge and work on your Being because these two combine to create understanding. All development depends entirely on your own efforts and motives. Sincerity is critical as is honesty. It is a lifetime process aimed at creating a psychology that is rightly ordered to be able to receive divine inspiration or what the Fourth Way calls higher influences.

It is called the Fourth Way in regard to the three other approaches to the inner development of Will. The first way is the way of the fakir; the way of the physical body developing body will. The second way is the way of the monk which forms an axis of religious devotion, love of God, creating emotional will. The third way is the way of the yogi, which develops mind will.

This system teaches that everyone is regarded as having three given bodies -- physical, emotional, intellectual -- and a potential fourth body which must be created by Will. A path which develops only one body is unbalanced. A fakir may develop enormous physical will and perhaps be able to hold his arms outstretched for years. Of what use is this? He has not developed his emotional body or his intellectual body and so with his will he can do nothing of value. It is nearly the same with the other two paths. The monk is undeveloped physically and intellectually. The yogi is undeveloped physically and emotionally. The developmental teaching of the Fourth Way works with all three given bodies simultaneously to produce Balanced Man who can develop Conscious Will which is the access to divine body.

The four bodies are called in Christian terminology the carnal, natural, spiritual and divine natures. In the Fourth Way, these are the first body, second body, third body, and fourth body.

The first body is the most external part, the physical body which experiences sensations. It is given to us already organized, but it functions mechanically by responding to external impressions.

The second body is the emotional body and is an unorganized mass of feelings and desires, constantly changing, subject to no direction, responding automatically. It is more internal than the first body.

The third body is the intellectual body which is the seat of thoughts and thinking functions. It is also an unorganized mass of changing thoughts stimulated randomly.

The fourth body is the divine body. It is accessible only by Will created in the ordering of the second and third bodies. Developing Conscious Will by organizing your three given bodies gives you access to your divine body or nature, which is inexpressible. If this is achieved, the fourth body then has existence and it possesses consciousness, individuality, and will. The fourth Will--Body is Master. It is the highest and most internal part of you.

The functioning of an undeveloped man is initiated by external life. His first body, physical body, experiences sensations which give rise to emotions in the second body which find expression in thoughts in the third body. In this case, there is no fourth body, no will-body, just a jumble of small, conflicting momentary wills stimulated by the unorganized emotions and thoughts. His functions are governed by changing sensations in external life.

In this system, developed Man is directed by consciousness in his divine body and obeys divine will. In this case, the most internal part (fourth body) is directing the functions of the other three bodies. The fourth body conscious awareness understands what any circumstance needs and the divine will directs thoughts in the third body regarding these needs which produces corresponding selfless emotions in the second body which creates appropriate actions in the first body. In this way, what is highest is generating actions with intentionality and the three given bodies are subject to it.

The acquisition of a Divine body is the same process as that of baptism. The Fourth Way is practical instruction on the process of this acquisition.

THE GENERAL STRUCTURE OF THE SYSTEM

There are three aspects of the general structure of the Fourth Way system as it was taught at Fontainebleau -- the cosmology, the movements, and the Work.

The Cosmology

There is much to be gained by studying the cosmology of the Fourth way. However, I would say to you at the beginning that one of the cornerstone ideas of this system is the admonition verify everything for yourself. The cosmology is a mind-expanding model of the universe. The study of it can impart a perspective of scale and relativity and stretch the mind dimensionally. Some of the ideas act as a shock of sorts, designed to awaken you a little or cause you to think differently about creation in general and your place and meaning in it. If you reflect on the ideas, you may begin to have a change in your understanding.

The Ray of Creation is the primary cosmological model about the ordering of the universe. All created things are ordered according to laws otherwise there would be only chaos -- disorder. This system teaches that the universe is living and evolving, seeking unity and consciousness. Its structure is represented in the Ray of Creation.

The Ray shows us seven levels of Creation, beginning with the Absolute, which is subject to only one law -- the law of its own will. The second level is the level of all possible starry systems or galaxies and it is under three laws. Each subsequent level is subject to the number of laws of the preceding level and in addition, that same number of laws at its own level. So the third level, which is the level of our Milky Way, is under three laws from the second level and three laws of its own, therefore six laws belong to that level. The fourth level is the level of our sun which is under twelve laws. The fifth is the level of the planets as one mass, under twenty-four laws. The sixth is the level of our earth, under forty-eight laws. The seventh is the level of our moon, under ninety-six laws.

The Ray of Creation teaches that all matter is energy condensing as it moves farther away from its source in the Absolute, becoming coarser and denser material. It teaches that our earth and the human beings on it appear far down in the Ray and are consequently subject to many laws; the laws of nature, the laws of physics, the law of accident, etc. It teaches that Man is a self-developing being created for a special purpose in the function of the Ray of Creation. For that reason, we have been given the free will to choose evolution. Gurdjieff:

There is only evolution and non-evolution. Actually, there is also degeneration which is certainly non-evolution, but it is not a static condition. It is possible also to lose the ability to become conscious through degeneration.

That special purpose in the Ray of Creation for which we are created, individually and collectively, is expressed in its simplest terms in the cosmology by the table of hydrogens. Our purpose can most elementally be put as transforming energies from coarser vibrations to finer vibrations.

The law of Seven or the Law of Octaves in the cosmology is a teaching about the ordering of creation on different levels -- in the macrocosm of the universe and in the microcosm of Man.

One of the most important points to understand in studying the Ray of Creation is that the nature of the Absolute is one thing -- perfect Goodness.

The Law of Three, sometimes called the Law of the Trinity, teaches that in every manifestation of anything in the universe, three forces must be present. They are 1) Active Force, 2) Passive Force, 3) Neutralizing Force. Active and Passive forces essentially cancel each other out and produce nothing. A third neutralizing force is necessary to bring the opposites into relationship in order to produce something.

The cosmology of the Fourth Way is mind-expanding and enlightening. It can give you a valuation for the magnitude of this teaching and a perspective on its aim, including ideological shocks that help to create moments of higher consciousness. In this system, it is taught that you must begin in the Work with the study of the cosmology and this can have validity for the above reasons. However, in doing so, you will find eventually that all of the cosmology cannot be verified and you are instructed not to take anything on faith. More importantly, whatever knowledge you can receive does not result in personal transformation. Even the most astute knowledge of the cosmology cannot produce a permanent transformation of consciousness, which is the whole aim of esoteric teaching.

The Movements

At the Institute in France, students participated in learning Sufi dances or movements. This physical exercise was practice in attention, discipline, cooperation, precision, perseverance, and more, including occupation for the students. The dances were performed in public to earn money for the Institute, as well. They are quite extraordinary. It is said that these movements, or dances, carry esoteric meaning. This may or may not be so, or may or may not be verifiable. In any case, the unavoidable fact is that just as intellectual knowledge of the Fourth Way cosmology doesn't produced transformation, neither do the movements.

In spite of this, many Fourth Way schools insist that the Movements must be practiced as part of the system, and in order to be balanced. This is a serious misinterpretation of the idea of balanced centers or balanced Man in this teaching. The only physical requirement for transformation of consciousness is brain function, so regardless of their relative value, the Movements are not necessary for transformation of mind. Nicoll: No amount of attention to the body will create transformation.

The Work

The psychological exercises and practices of the Fourth Way are the Work of the system. They are specifically designed to be used in your daily life experiences. They are aimed at self-knowledge, growing authenticity and becoming conscious. This is the transformation that esotericism refers to and the psychological Work is the means for attaining it.

The ideas and exercises and practices of the Work are meant to build something up inside you that lifts you into a higher level of consciousness. Nicoll: The knowledge of this Work is of a kind that can act on Being and as a result give rise to understanding. This action can only take place using the force of your personal efforts in practicing the Work. Applying the ideas to yourself with sincerity and diligence is effort -- Work. This is doing the Work -- being in the Work. Many students think and say that they are in the Work simply because they are studying the Fourth Way system. This is not so. You have to do the Work in order to be in the Work.

LEVELS OF CONSCIOUSNESS

The premise for assuming that there can be a developmental system lies in understanding the idea of different levels in an individual. All of the ideas of the Work are based on understanding that different levels of consciousness exist. Therefore, movement from one level to another level is possible. Nicoll: As he is, Man serves the purposes of nature and nothing else is necessary in regards to his life. But he can put himself under different influences if he chooses. He can change his level of consciousness and consequently attract different circumstances according to his level.

In this system there are said to be seven levels of consciousness consisting of four states which belong to three different kinds of Man existing at different levels.

Man # 1, 2, and 3 all share the first two states equally. First State is resting sleep, literal sleep with dreams. Second State is called Waking State in which you walk and talk and act in life mechanically. The Work calls Second State Sleep as well, because it functions automatically without consciousness.

At this level of consciousness, there is only the darkness of being asleep. No help is possible because higher influences can only reach down as far as the Third State of Consciousness. This is what the system teaches, but it would be more accurate to say that Man asleep -- mechanical Man (numbers 1, 2, and 3) cannot perceive the finer vibrations coming from higher consciousness because of the coarse nature of his Being. The Absolute can reach where it wills but mechanical Man turns a deaf ear.

Man # 4 is at the Third State of Consciousness. He is beginning to awaken through the practice of Self-Observation and Self-Remembering. He has some degree self-awareness and Real I.
Man # 4 is called Balanced Man which in general terms means a man functioning properly. Balanced Man has organized his centers (or bodies) -- the functions of his psychology. He is able to remain upright in the center of the swinging pendulum of life events and circumstances. Achieving this state requires long term, sincere, hard psychological Work. Real inner Work. But the right efforts

made for the right motives will produce real inner change. From the level of Man # 4, influences, inspiration and understanding can reach him, light is present and help is possible.

Man numbers 5, 6, and 7 live in Fourth State -- Objective Consciousness. These three are called Conscious Man, Man Awake. Light is present and help is available. At this level, a man can see things as they really are.

Conscious Man has understanding and perspective, intentionally developed Consciousness and Being, active Real Conscience and the Will to do. Conscious Man is authentic and living out his meaning and purpose in Gods will. He is guided by divine inspiration, spiritual direction, objective Truth, real Conscience, objective consciousness, and goodness above all things. Conscious Man is incapable of violence.

SLEEP

Lets look at an example of mechanical Man, that is, Man asleep, Man #1, 2 and 3, which means all of us.

Lets take the ordinary circumstances in the daily life of an ordinary man. Lets say he is married and has a dog and a job. He wakes in the morning to the sound of the alarm clock and immediately wishes he could sleep longer. Resignation accompanies bringing his feet to the floor. His shower revives him and he remembers that today is Friday. Relieved and happy about the weekend, he begins to imagine the activities he plans. While he is thinking about a pleasant event, he gets soap in his eye and immediately anger flairs. Perhaps he swears or growls or some such. When he steps out of the shower with his stinging eye, he finds the dog scratching and whining at the bathroom door. He irritably wonders why his wife hasn't let the dog out yet. He can't do it right now. The dog will have to wait, he says to himself with impatience. He hurries to finish his preparations, dropping his toothbrush and nicking his chin while his frustration builds. His mind returns repeatedly to the special occasion on the weekend and he imagines conversations and scenarios where he is the center of attention or where he is appreciated, flattered, and of course always right. Or he worries about who will be there, how they will treat him, whether he will make a good impression, if they will like him or embarrass him. Dressed, he comes out to find that the dog has gone and he is irritable again, thinking how he hurried and cut himself shaving only to find that it was unnecessary. The smell of coffee attracts him and his first sip brings him a wave of pleasure. His wife comes in and they share a warm greeting. He is noticing how nice the weather is when she lets the dog back in. The dog jumps up and his hot coffee sloshes over the edge of his cup, burning his hand and staining his shirt. He yells at the dog and explodes with anger over his shirt. He stalks from the room. Changing his shirt means changing ties and now he can barely manage it, what with his burned fingers, nicked chin, and stinging eye. He swears he is going to take that dog to obedience school. He never wanted it in the first place, it was her idea. She can take the dog to school. Now he is running late, so he skips breakfast, says a hurried goodbye to his wife, and heads out for work. Traffic is light and his favorite music is on, and it reminds him of sentimental times passed. Out of the blue, he remembers that he left his paperwork by the bedside instead of in his briefcase. He smacks the wheel with his hand and curses aloud. He has to return home and he will be late for sure now. He worries, he blames the dog, his wife, the shampoo, his life.

This man believes, as does every individual, that he is fully conscious, that he acts from his own volition and is perfectly aware of himself and of what he is doing. The Work says that a man functioning at this level is a stimulus-response organism reacting to life enslaved to his mechanical responses. He functions with no awareness or intentionality and he is asleep to this fact, unconscious of his state.

This is Sleep (Waking State, Second State). Everyone functions in this manner automatically, creating the chaos, suffering and violence in the world.

The idea that everyone is asleep is a shock that can help

to change your thinking. However, the awareness that you yourself are Asleep is a shock of awakening. This awareness you can only gain through personal Verification.

AWAKENING

The idea of awakening from this Sleep is to grow in consciousness and be able to act with intentionality instead of only reacting mechanically. The chief obstacle to awakening from this condition is that each person imagines that he already possesses full consciousness and self-awareness so he doesn't need it, doesn't seek it, isn't interested. Each person believes that they act with cognizance and that they possess the will to do whatever they choose to do.

The Work tells us that this is an illusion and that the illusion that you are already properly conscious is part of the condition of being asleep. Note please that the Work does not tell you that life is an illusion (which can make you insane). It tells you that your subjective view of it is an illusion.

People don't act. They react. From the beginning of their life, each person is reacting to the circumstances that come to them and this is the only way it can be. But the mechanical, automatic stimulus-response organism, which means each of us, is also created as a self-developing organism. We can evolve in consciousness by way of specific intentional efforts.

ESSENCE, REAL I, AND BEING

You were born with a unique self that has a few innate qualities which are observable. As an infant, you were either primarily active or passive and you had either a positive disposition or a negative disposition predominantly. There are other idiosyncratic attributes present at birth that are more subtle, but the point is that you are born with a totally unique self already present. In the Work, this is called your Essence. It contains your reason for being.

As an infant, your essence is somewhat like a clean slate. It has unique characteristics and disposition, but as your essence is influenced by its experience in your environment, your personality is formed around it. Personality is acquired to enable you to interact with life and survive because self-preservation is the primary directive. In human development, that directive translates into gaining power over your environment in order to get your needs met so that you can survive which is, after all, the first precondition necessary for any other possibility.

So Essence is the more internal part of you and the more authentic part, but it is overlaid with a personality which may not express your essence at all. Remember that personality was formed around essence via your subjective experience of your life and its events over which you had no control. Essence can only develop in life up to a certain point when personality must take over. It remains undeveloped and powerless unless it is intentionally developed through the Work. The intention in the Work is to develop Essence until it has the power to direct your personality. This process revolves around making your Acquired Personality passive so that essence can become active. If this process is successful and essence develops, Real I emerges.

Real I is Master. Everyone has Real I which will manifest developed Essence in True Personality, but it also must be gradually reached through the Work. It exists within you at the level of Self-Remembering, the Third State of consciousness. The Work teaches exercises and practices which help to bring Real I into presence. The practice of Self-Observation informs and illuminates Real I and carries a taste of it because they are connected at the same level of consciousness.

Personality is the most external part of you. Behind Acquired Personality is Essence, and behind Essence lies Real I. Psychologically speaking, Essence is internal to personality and Real I is internal to Essence. Real I is your highest self. It is the truth of your Being.

What the Work calls your Being is roughly the nature of your character. Everyone possesses Being to one degree or another. Being exists in scale that is on different levels and it can be developed. For example, the Being of an honorable man is greater or above the Being of a criminal man. In the very beginning of the Work, you are asked to work in two areas of yourself -- work on Knowledge and work on Being. That is because it is this special esoteric knowledge applied to your Being which produces understanding and it is said in this Work that understanding is the most powerful force you can develop. The development of consciousness is inseparable from the development of Being. They go hand in hand.

One of the elements in the scale of Being is that different levels are discontinuous with each other, like parallel telephone lines between two poles. The events you encounter on one level of Being may not exist on another level which has its own different events. Nicoll: The level of Being awaiting you just above your present line, which is your evolution, your inner development, your inner growth, is discontinuous with your present level, just as one rung of a ladder is not continuous with the next. You have to jump.

The most important idea in the Work about Being is that your Being attracts your life.

ACQUIRED (FALSE) PERSONALITY

As was said, Essence interacts with life and personality is formed from these infinite idiosyncratic factors. Personality forms around Essence as a means of interacting with life and this is absolutely necessary. It forms according to laws that apply to everyone. In other words, its formulation is ordered.

The Work calls this formation of personality the first education. It is referred to in this system as False Personality and it is indeed false. I find the term Acquired Personality somewhat clearer and more specific, less condemning.

Personality in general can be described as a collection of habits. Habits of thinking -- thinking about the same things in the same ways; habits of feeling -- recurring emotions, repetitive emotional states; habits of talking -- repeating the same stories, the same phrases, the same words. You have habits of attitudes and of opinions. You have habits of the physical body -- posture, facial expressions, tensions, movements, body language; habits of Being and habitual ways of responding to life events. You acquired all of these habits by imitation, by opposition, by family and cultural and community influences. That is, life influences in which you had no choice, therefore these habits are not You. You are not your personality.

Your personality renders life to you according to its unique shape or formulation, automatically. You have an attitude about something, an opinion about another thing, you have feelings and thoughts and these things compose your experience. Yet all of these habits that make up your personality do not express your Essence or your Real I. You may experience this sometimes as the feeling of being a phony or being unknown to yourself.

Essence has to be intentionally developed as well as Real I. These two aspects do not evolve mechanically. They evolve only with the personal efforts of attention and intentionality taught in esotericism, in the Work.

One of the primary teachings about personality is that it has an illusion of unity. Ouspensky: The illusion of unity or oneness is created in Man first, by the sensation of one physical body, by his name....and third, by a number of mechanical habits which are implanted in him by education or acquired by imitation. Having always the same physical sensations, hearing always the same name, and noticing in himself the same habits and inclinations he had before, he believes himself to be always the same.

The Work teaches that, in reality, Man is a disorganized mass of Is with no permanence. Each thought, feeling, sensation, like or dislike is an I. Unconnected, contradictory and even opposite Is in you say I as if each speaks for the whole of you. This is called the Doctrine of Is and although it may sound incomprehensible at first, it is easily verified and critical to your development. You can observe within yourself the turning wheel of Is, each a thought or an emotion, a desire or a sensation. Man is a Multiplicity, not a unity. There is no single controlling I or will. Each I has its own small temporary will which vanishes when the next I is dominant.

The recognition of your Multiplicity marks a critical stage in the Work process. It feels very unstable to see your lack of identity and can induce a kind of psychological vertigo that is frightening. Ironically, it is by way of this Multiplicity that you find the opportunity for intentional change and real stability.

The Work teaches you how to recognize and choose and nurture the Is in you that belong to higher consciousness or Real I and how to become detached from Is that are harmful or do not express your Real I. In this way, the Work works in your psychology on your personality.

But Man commonly takes himself as one I and has a picture in his mind of himself as his personality. This is his imaginary I. It is a cloak put on by each I in turn.

There is another very significant teaching about personal-

ity in the Work which I would like to make particularly clear. There is a level of development in personality called Good Householder. This means a person who does his duty in life, lives responsibly to himself and in the world, without criminality or perversion. Only a person who has reached this stage called Good Householder is fit for the Work. If you cannot live a decent ordinary life, then you have no chance of success in the extraordinary Work.
Nicoll: Let us again recapitulate the teaching about Being. First, a man must be in life and have dealt with life and reached some adequate position in life and knowledge of life and so be a Good Householder, capable of dealing with the ordinary difficulties and problems of human existence -- that is, the Work is not for people who seek to escape from the normal burdens of life. It is for normal decent people and starts from that level of Being. It is very important that everyone should understand this.

THE PSYCHOLOGY OF POSSIBLE EVOLUTION

The development or evolution that is possible for a person on this earth, in their lifetime, is psychological. Remember that Man is created on the earth as a self-evolving being capable of self-generated psychological change -- development. This Work which begins with self-knowledge is called self-evolution because it is only through sincere efforts intentionally made by yourself that the possibility of evolution exists. It is in and through the energy of the effort to Work that evolution happens. Each person must make their own efforts in order to evolve. Only personal inner Work effort produces the force for evolution. This process in the Work will take you from self-interested psychology to self-transcendent psychology. Awakening from a sleeping mechanical psychology to an intentional conscious psychology is your destiny. It is what each of us is here to do. The fact that this Teaching exists is hard proof of Gods unconditional Love reaching down to us even in our insignificance; His very personal Love for each of us individually and equally.

LECTURE 3

The Work Terminology

1. SLEEP:
The Work teaches that every human being walking around in their daily life does so in such a subjective state of mind, at such a low level of consciousness, that it can be likened to a state of unawareness as intensely unreal as the state of actual sleep. This condition of Sleep applies to the whole of humanity and to each person. The Work teaches a system for Awakening from Sleep.
This state of Sleep, which applies to the psychological condition of every person, is also called Second State or Waking State. In this automatically functioning mode, you interact in the world, in your life, by reacting to everything according to the formation of your psychology. You believe that you are your personality and that your subjective opinions and attitudes and beliefs are right and true. You therefore invest yourself, give your identity to every response you have, remaining unaware that you are responding mechanically to the stimuli from life.

2. LEVELS OF CONSCIOUSNESS:
The Work teaches that there are different levels of Con-

sciousness, beginning with the state of literal physical sleep, which is called First State, to the Waking state of living your daily life in the world, which is called in the Work, Sleep, or Second State, all the way to a fully evolved consciousness characterized by permanent unity.

It teaches that everyone lives their life in First and Second States, but that other levels are available as well. Eventually it comes down to choosing what level you want to live at and express -- to which influences you choose to put yourself under.

Fully developed consciousness in a person, which means psychologically evolved, is characterized by Unity and Purity in their Being. It expresses their uniqueness purified, living in a permanent state of spiritual development, which is humble and self-transcendent and receptive to Divine influence.

The Work is a methodology for raising your level of consciousness, intentionally. That is why it is called self-evolution.

3. POSSIBLE PSYCHOLOGICAL EVOLUTION:
The Work maintains that a person can intentionally raise their level of Consciousness upwards through the ideas and practices and exercises present in the psycho-

transformational teaching of the Fourth Way.

Since there are different levels of Consciousness, change from one level to another is possible. Development is possible. Development means evolution.

This development does not happen automatically or mechanically in life. It requires intentional and specific efforts from the individual. It manifests as a permanent change in a person to a new level of Being, a new quality of character, a new depth of understanding, a new emotional perspective.

It is called self-evolution because the development is built upon your own sincere efforts. You need to know what you are doing in the Work, and what you are aiming at. Then you can do the Work willingly, which is essential, aware and committed to your aim. Therefore, your Work efforts will build something new in you. Real change is possible. Remember that the direction of evolution is upwards.

This system teaches that every human being comes into the world with a particular kind of essence nature which is unique to the individual. This essential nature interacts with its environment and a personality is produced that is subject to many variables. The outcome -- Acquired Personality -- is the result of what the Work calls the first education. It is a necessary development intended to create a means with which to interact in life responsibly. It is the second level of Consciousness. It is not the end of potential development, however it is as far as most will go.

The Work is sometimes called the second education. It can only take hold in a person who has a mature Acquired Personality. This is called being a Good Householder, which simply put means being a responsible person in your life, to yourself and to the world as well. A person in this position can use the Work, this second education, to reconstruct an authentic Being, true to their essence nature . You can build a structure psychologically that can lift you above the mechanical stimulus-response level of Consciousness. Building this structure through personal efforts of practicing the Work will lead you into a new level of Consciousness and growth in Being which is the Psychological Evolution possible for humankind.

4. AWAKENING:

Awakening means raising your level of consciousness from an automatic stimulus-response mechanical level to that higher level of awareness possible within you. It means changing from a self-interest motivated person to a self-transcendent conscious person with an evolved level of Being. It means real change in the nature of a human being. It does not just happen. Each person has to create this change through specific Work practices and diligent efforts over a long time period.

5. REAL I:

It is Real I that is awakened by Self-Awareness. It is the who you remember in the act of full Self-Remembering. Everyone has Real I within them. It is the truth of your Being, but it remains inactive and powerless behind Acquired Personality. During the course of the Work, as you eliminate the Wrong Work in your Acquired Personality, Real I grows in presence. Self-Observation stands in front of Real I and informs it during its development. The growth of Real I is directly connected to the emergence of Buried Conscience as well. Self-Observation informs Real I, Conscience shapes it. True Personality expresses it.

6. TRUE PERSONALITY:

Real I expresses True Personality, which is your purified Real Self. True Personality is authentic and comfortable and flexible and is Externally Considerate. True Personality manifests humility. Your own personal sacrifice of mechanical self-interest creates the space where Consciousness and Being can be transformed and True Personality is revealed.

7. CONSCIENCE:

The Work teaches that there are two kinds of Conscience -- Acquired Conscience and Real Conscience. Acquired Conscience is different in different cultures and places and times and in individuals. The fact that it changes means that it is not objective or an expression of Unified Conscience. What may be seen as cause for pride in one era or culture may be cause for shame in another. Nicoll: Acquired Conscience is based on self-love, and self-love is based on fear.

Everyone also possesses Real Conscience, but it is buried and weak and nearly inaudible. Real Conscience is the same in everyone and those who have developed it understand each other because they understand the same things through the enlightenment of Conscience. Nicoll: The growth of consciousness and the growth of Conscience must necessarily go hand in hand.
The Work teaches that Real Conscience doesn't have enough force for action. The process of purifying the Emotional Center, which is the foundational labor in the Work, reveals a greater degree of Conscience. Your Conscience grows in the Work through Understanding and the consequences of purification. It develops correspondingly with Consciousness and level of Being. Conscience is connected to spiritual direction, it recognizes Truth and Goodness and it helps to formulate Real I. It is active in discernment and in choosing self-transcendence.

8. BEING:

Roughly speaking, your Being is the quality of your character. Your level of Being is an expression of the nature of your psychology. Being is mechanical and present in everyone to different degrees. Being can be developed and indeed must develop in the Work along with Consciousness or there will be no right result from this process. You cannot possess a higher level of Consciousness which has been purified of negativity and selfishness and at the same time maintain a level of action in the world that express no change in Being. The nature of your character -- Being -- must be correspondingly transformed to a higher level, or Consciousness remains theoretical and has no power, no force. In the Work, Being is Goodness.

9. DIVIDED ATTENTION:

In order to practice the most important exercise in the Work, that of Self-Observation, you must first learn how to divide your attention, or rather that you can divide your attention. The idea of seeing a tree, and seeing yourself seeing a tree, is only part of the equation. You must realize that your attention is constantly engaged, moving from one event to another. Whether you are active in the world or not, your attention is engaged in a constant string of reactions to your life. Your thoughts, your feelings, your words, your actions, your attitudes, your opinions, your likes and dislikes, your moods or states are always taking all of your attention in one direction -- projecting these things into your life. This projecting has energy and it all flows outward like a twenty-four hour radio station emitting a constant noise.

When you use your divided attention to practice Self-Observation, you are creating an interior vantage point that can view all of the noise. It can observe both your actions in life and your underlying feelings and motives. Dividing your Attention in this manner takes Conscious effort. You have to make a Conscious choice and use intentionality in Dividing your attention to create the vantage point of Observing I. Simply learning the exercise of Divided Attention goes nowhere until you use that division to practice Self-Observation by dividing yourself into an observed side and an observing side.

10. SELF-OBSERVATION:

The practice of Self-Observation is the most fundamental exercise in the Work. You can't know yourself unless you observe yourself. Self-knowledge in the Work sense is essential for change and development.

Once you can divide your attention so that you have a new vantage point in addition to your normal awareness;

and when what you can see from this new psychological position is your self acting in the world and your own psychological condition as well, then you have begun. This is somewhat like learning to pat your head and rub your tummy at the same time, psychologically speaking. It takes attention, practice, and adjustments.

You do this observing from a new vantage point that you must make within yourself, from which you can see all of your behavior and the psychology which creates it. Nicoll: ...First you must try to see everything in yourself in a given moment. The emotional state, thoughts, sensations, intentions, posture, movements, tone of voice, facial expressions, and so on. This vantage point or new perspective is called Observing I. It is directed at your psychology and it shines the light of Awareness into the psychological mechanics which have been functioning in the dark.

Practicing Self-Observation must be refined as you proceed. Most importantly, you must learn to do it without becoming negative because of what you observe in yourself. This does not mean do not recognize what is right from what is wrong. It means do not get caught up in an emotional response to what you observe. If you do, you have lost your perspective and are stuck in an emotional state that will obstruct your progress and your ability to see with clarity.

Sincerity, being able to be honest with yourself, and focus

are part of the nature of practicing Self-Observation correctly. You must accept beforehand that you have to be able to see what is wrong in order to change it. If you remain unenlightened concerning something within you that is preventing your development, then again you are stuck and cannot change. So you must be willing to observe all that is in you. You must practice Self-Observation frequently, diligently, tenaciously, sincerely, and uncritically.

11. VERIFICATION:

One of the first tenets of the Work is verify everything for yourself. You may need to have an open mind to grasp a Work idea, but you are not asked to accept anything that you cannot verify. This of course means that you have to DO the Work. The result will give you Verification. Verification is experiential understanding and it lives in your Work memory and gives it substance.

12. SELF-REMEMBERING:

Of all of the Work practices, Self-Remembering is the least understood and the most incorrectly practiced. One of the reasons is because Self-Remembering has many degrees and forms. Giving yourself the First Conscious Shock is a form of Self-Remembering as is remembering the Work ideas, and remembering your Aim. The practice of Self-Observation and of becoming present are also lesser forms of practicing Self-Remembering because they bring the Work to the point of incoming impressions and carry a taste of Real I.

Self-Remembering is making an effort to recollect what your essential Being is, your Real I, within the context of Scale and Relativity. It is a paradoxical experience in that you feel your nothingness and your uniqueness, and you also feel connected to all of Creation, an integral part of all that is. In a full state of Self-Remembering, Real I is who is present.

You can reach up to this higher state in your consciousness of Self-Remembering and sometimes touch what you are reaching for briefly. This is so that you can know and verify that this higher state exists within you. It is through your personal Work that you can develop the ability to Remember yourself in the full sense and become your Real I.

13. NEGATIVE EMOTIONS:

One of the largest areas of study in the Work is the nature and activity of Negative Emotions. There are many good reasons to begin practicing Self-Observation by observing Negative Emotions. They have a strong recognizable energy and quality, they are preponderant, they lead you around and waste your energy, they obstruct conscious development because they anchor you to the lowest level of consciousness. They also lie.

The other good reason to begin with observing Negative Emotions is because the Work asks you to stop giving expression to all of your Negative Emotions from the beginning of your Work. In doing so, you will learn many profound truths about yourself. First you will have to notice your Negative Emotions after you have learned what to observe. This, you will find far too easy. You will be shocked to observe in yourself how many Negative Emotions you have and how they dominate and taint your life. Then you will discover to your horror, that you can only barely, sometimes, keep from giving expression to them. You will see how Negative Emotions arise against your will and intention; how quickly you are swept away by them, and how you justify having them. It is a great inner struggle and it will take time and development before you can transcend your Negative Emotions instead of just trying to repress them.

The following are some of the Negative Emotions that you are asked by the Work to observe in yourself: annoyance, criticizing, self-pity, impatience, malice, vengeance, frustration, complaining, feeling offended, irritability, envy, sadness, restlessness, boredom, depression, anger, smugness, indignation, hopelessness, shame, nervousness, melancholy, insecurity, embarrassment, dissatisfaction, and more.

Each of these is examined as you observe them. They are studied and worked against and eliminated. For example, if you observe that you are feeling annoyed, examine why. If the answer is because -- whatever -- is annoying you, then you are observing in the wrong direction. The source of the negativity is not outside you. Your Negative Emotions are ALWAYS your own responsibility. Virtually no external circumstance can MAKE you negative. There is always another way. With growth in the Work you become able to choose not to become negative. You will see upon observation that you are Negative because your circumstances don't meet the requirements you have. In the Work, you will learn how to release your requirements, not how to make your circumstances satisfy them. You will learn to accept not being satisfied by way of working against Negative Emotions. This state of acceptance detaches you from the dissatisfaction of not having your requirements met. Most of your Negative Emotions come from dissatisfaction. In studying them, you will find that the dissatisfaction is the product of having requirements that are not fulfilled. You will see that behind your requirements lie a bevy of self-interested motives and false presuppositions.

The Work will tell you to look at your Negative Emotions and identify them. Then you must look behind them to the place in your psychology where they originate. You can only do these two things by the means of practicing Self-Observation. Through Self-Observation you will see that the emotions of suspicion, jealousy, and insecurity, for example, are generated by fear. While the emotions are very real and the needs feel very strong, all of them are produced by self-interest...you want, you need, you feel, you don't want, etc.

The Work teaches you to transcend self-interest, consequently Negative Emotions have no source and cease to exist. Getting rid of Negative Emotions is the process of purification necessary for development to Higher Consciousness through the Work. Negativity uses and wastes your limited energy and attention and obstructs your path. While you are in a negative state you are effectively cut off from higher emotions, the psychological place you are aiming at. Negative Emotions are the lowest levels of Consciousness in action, the most mechanical level. In order to gain in Consciousness or raise your level of Being, you must become purified of Negative Emotions.

14. MECHANICALNESS:
According to the Work, everything that happens on earth happens mechanically, dictated by cosmic laws that cannot be verified. Mechanicalness, however, can easily be verified and Worked with.

Negative Emotions are the most mechanical level of functioning in a human being, and this can be verified by observing them. Negativity is very easy to observe. All it takes is seeing how a particular event makes you feel a Negative Emotion in response, repeated (for example, driving on the highway always makes you feel anxious) to verify that Negative Emotions and states are mechanical responses. You will notice that you become angry if you feel you are not being treated well enough and that you join in gossip, or you hear yourself lying or pretending or complaining, exaggerating, criticizing, slandering, etc. You notice how a negative topic introduced into conversation about bad weather, health, kids, bosses, doctors, etc -- will generate energy and everyone will join in telling their experience, creating a momentary wild fire of negative energy. This observation verifies that Negative Emotions are contagious.

Everyone is functioning according to their own personal agenda. Everyone seeks satisfaction, attention, appreciation, and acceptance. Everyone becomes negative when they suffer, when they don't get what they want. And it is all mechanical, that is, belonging to the lowest level of consciousness which is response to stimulus without awareness. All of the emotions in Acquired Personality are mechanical responses. That applies to each person and the whole of Humanity as well.

15. ACQUIRED PERSONALITY:
Conventionally, the term used in the Fourth Way is False Personality. There is no disagreement with the accuracy

of the term false if there is no condemnation in it. However, the term ACQUIRED Personality is far more specific and informative with no condemnation implied. Nonetheless, Acquired Personality is unquestionably false.

The Work teaches that ever person is born into the world with an innate nature and unique being, and also with a purpose. This is called Essence. It is basically the who of your Being. But, since as an infant you are also a blank slate, so to speak, your experience shapes your Personality to a great degree. As your Essence interacts with the experience of your existence, the nature of your personality is gradually formed and acquired. This is necessary for normal development. But it is a limited level of development. There is a potential level of a higher Self available. The Work teaches you how to develop this potential higher Self.

In the formation of Acquired Personality, attitudes and habitual patterns of feeling and thinking and acting are created by imitation and environmental influences. This kind of personality formation is automatic and common to everyone while remaining idiosyncratic. It is not created purposefully or even with your consent. Your Acquired Personality is rather like the result of everything that was done to you during its formation. It is up to each individual adult to choose a path of self-development, to have Consciousness and authenticity, integrity and self-transcendence, and express their Real I in True Personality.

You have to observe your Acquired Personality in order to discern what is false and what is true to your Real I, your highest Self. In this Work process, your Conscience becomes more active and is able to discern between good and bad, right and wrong, true and false with increasing clarity.

The transformation of Acquired Personality is basically reconstructing your psychology to express your Real I, your highest Consciousness and Being. It means changing from a self-interested psychology to a self-transcendent psychology. The process is difficult because it involves deconstructing the ego, which is painful to the ego. It is destabilizing and therefore requires great strength of character and a strong need to change and have understanding in order to grow in the Work.

Acquired Personality is who you think you are. It is sometimes called your Imaginary I. It is defined by your attitudes, opinions, feelings, likes and dislikes, imitations, habitual responses and habitual ways of thinking and feeling and acting. It is the Acquired Personality that acts most mechanically automatically without consciousness or intentionality, churning out responses (energy) to stimuli according to the formation of your psychology. In the Work, all of what is false or wrong or negative in the

Acquired Personality is observed and studied, worked against and separated from. This means long-term efforts.

16. IMAGINARY I:

Imaginary I is your identity according to the pictures you have of yourself as your personality. If someone were to ask you what kind of person you are, your answer would be a description of Imaginary I. You perhaps think you are a good old boy, or a loyal patriot, or an avant-garde artist, or an intellectual, or a fair and honest person, or a social activist, etc. These characteristics belong to Acquired Personality. They are not you.

Imaginary I has the illusion of unity but in reality it is the constantly changing mass of all of the Is. There is no one permanent I in control. But a man has one body and one name and a personality made of imaginary pictures, which leads him to believe that he is always the same -- this Imaginary I.

17. BUFFERS:

Buffers are like a psychological appliance created by Man in the formation of his personality to absorb the shock of contradictions in himself; in his views and in his words, his thoughts and emotions. They take the place of the

Real Conscience we have as small children, in order to reconcile us with acquired Conscience. Ouspensky: Buffers make things easy for us. They prevent us from seeing what we are really doing and saying. If Man could see all of the dire contradictions in himself all at once he would feel that he is mad. Gurdjieff: He must either destroy the contradictions or cease to feel and see them. . . . . Buffers help a man not to feel Conscience.

18. SELF-LOVE:
Everything in the Personality is based on self-love, that is self-interest, and this is the only way that it can be. Self-love is based on fear. Basic urges motivate actions that express a need for power or control over your environment and circumstances. These urges arise from the instinct for self-preservation and are necessary in the first education.

If you think of self-love as the source of self-interested motives and you know that you have a mechanical Acquired Personality, then regardless of its nature it is all based on self-love since it is created to serve the self. Self-love will pollute your good actions with pride and merit-seeking. It will lead most seekers down a path that teaches them that development means the ability to get everything they want, that the manifestation of your desires means fulfillment. Self-love seeks attention by any means. It talks about itself and needs to be in the right, insists that it is right. Self-love exaggerates to flatter and inflate its good appearance to others and it takes offense very easily. All of these forms of Wrong Work arising from self-love are dealt with through Work practices and ideas and they lose power, and eventually they cease to be the motives that generate the actions of your Personality.

19. IMAGINATION AND PICTURES:
Imagination, which can seem to be a benign, insubstantial force actually has great power in your psychology. Your imagination is assisted by your Acquired Personality in forming Pictures that you have of yourself in your mind, things that you believe about yourself, and imaginary perceptions about what others think of you.

The truth is that imagination is actually completely insubstantial. It is imaginary. But the power and reign your psychology allows it fills it with force.

It is primarily the Imaginary Pictures that you have of yourself about what kind of person you are, that the Work deals with. This is no trifling matter. Your Imaginary Pictures are the expression of what you are identified with in your Acquired Personality and they are entrenched in who you think you are.

Directed, creative imagination is not what is being referred to here. The Work speaks about mechanical

Imagination which is involved in most Wrong Work and perpetuates the consequential psychological malfunctions.

20. JUSTIFICATION:
Self-Justification is one of the most powerful forces which keeps us asleep. It is the activity of buffers. Always putting yourself in the right means staying in Sleep, not changing. Justification subtly alters things in the memory, emphasizing some and leaving others out. In other words, it lies. It is very important to the Acquired Personality which is based on self-love and needs to receive visible approval in order to maintain the Picture that Acquired Personality wants to present.

When you begin to observe Negative Emotions, your immediate response will be justifying them. You will feel quite right about being negative, placing the blame outside of yourself and you will feel relieved of the responsibility you have regarding Negative Emotions. This particular Wrong Work is easily recognizable and while it is hard to deal with in Work terms, it is something definite that you can observe and use in practicing the Work.

21. LYING:
There are so many forms of lying that they constitute an almost continuous condition of lying in our psychology. Lying is a great support in Justification and is always pre-

sent in Negative Emotions. But every form of dishonesty is also lying. If you exaggerate your attributes to make a good impression, you are lying. When you pretend to have interest in or sympathy with or understanding of or knowledge about something, when in reality you do not, then you are lying. You lie about your thoughts, your feelings, your motives, your intentions, your whereabouts, your activities, your income, your position, your merit, your success, your character, your nature, your interests, your aims. Most of all, you lie to yourself about who you are and in believing you have consciousness and unity.

It is hard to discern lying since it can be so subtle and insidious, but it has a particular quality or taste in the psychology that also becomes recognizable. When you are seeking Truth, it becomes very easy to discard lying once you start to recognize it. It plays a large part in all Wrong Work because Wrong Work involves Negative Emotions which always lie.

22. KEEPING ACCOUNTS:

Keeping accounts is specific Work language for what is basically holding a grudge against a person or even against life. When you keep an account against someone, you have a memory about them filled with all of the actions for which you resent them. If you have a long-term relationship in such a case, you will remember only what validates your ill will and all of the times they offended you in some way. Careful reflection will show you that lying is active and that the underlying feeling behind keeping an account is one of feeling that you haven't been treated properly so you didn't get your due. Therefore, the other person owes you. Or you may feel that life owes you, that you have never received the right opportunities or the good breaks, the worthy circumstances you deserve. These are some of the actions of Internal Considering.

23. COMPLAINING:
Complaining is like the background noise of your psychology. Once you start observing it, you will be shocked to find how much time you spend complaining, sometimes out loud, most often in your thoughts. Keeping accounts is a kind of complaining. Complaining is also full of lies. It is a one angled, tunnel vision, ungratified self-interested point of view.

Throughout your day, you will complain associatively about a number of things. Perhaps you start off each morning with the internal complaint of being tired. You can observe throughout the day complaining about your physical condition, traffic, your job, your boss, your spouse, your kids, the weather, fatigue, overwork, lack of appreciation. You can observe dissatisfaction (which is complaining) with your circumstances, your finances, your appearance, your position, your possessions, your relationships, what you have, what you don't have, how you feel, whether you are satisfied, gratified and comfortable. All of these are also forms of complaining.

Complaining is easy to observe, it arises from self-interested psychology that is constantly obsessed with being satisfied. It includes always only looking at the negative side of things and the background noise it forms is a constant stream of Inner Talking about your dissatisfaction with your life. Once you posses Scale and Relativity and some degree of developed Consciousness, you will see the pathetic nature of constantly complaining about not getting your way or having what you want, and how something so seemingly innocuous and justifiable can effectively obstruct transformation and Growth through the Work.

24. SONG SINGING:
Song singing is a specific Work term referring to an habitual set of complaining Is that repeat themselves in your psychology, the nature of which is something like woe is me. It may begin with an experience in the present, but that experience can trigger a set of Is that say the same thing to you over and over again throughout your lifetime. They are very familiar emotional states that have a descending quality. An example would be: your alarm doesn't go off, you wake up late and are immedi-

ately hurried, irritated, and you begin thinking Why does my alarm go on the fritz today when I need to be at work early? Why do things like that always happen to me? It seems like every time I have an important occasion, I'm plagued with problems that day. You would think I could get a break just once and not have to deal with any extra hassles on an important day. But no, the harder I try, the more difficulty I have. It seems like bad luck is just chasing me down, running me over and I can't get away from it. If this keeps up, Ill never be a success. What am I talking about, Ill never be a success anyway. Its useless. This is ridiculous. I'm tired of trying. I'm tired of failing. I don't know how to get what I want and I'm never going to be happy.

Very often, these kinds of songs will be about your difficult childhood or your painful relationships or your unsatisfied vocation. But they always say the same thing and it is always a sad song about your sad circumstances and your unhappy life. You will recognize them easily due to familiarity. After paying attention long enough to know what these emotional habits express, the only way to deal with them is to practice Inner Silence in relation to them.

25. INNER TALKING:
Inner talking is the vehicle for complaining and song singing and keeping accounts and justifying, among other things. It is the normal functioning of your psychology to be constantly engaged in either external or internal talk-

ing, or both at the same time. The subject matter varies, but the monologue is your constant commentary on your experiences and feelings and thoughts. Generally speaking, there is a negative quality as in the above examples, but there are many kinds of inner talking. It can be imagination, fantasy, day dreaming, or even positive subject matter and emotions as well. Through Self-Observation, you will find that Inner talking is going on inside you at all times.

In the Work, you will need to know what to make silent and to see whatever real perception may be present. In any case, Inner Talking is primarily an obstruction to receptivity. If you are full of comments, opinions, attitudes, and responses, how can hear from Higher Consciousness?

26. INTERNAL CONSIDERING:
Internal Considering refers to an enormously prevalent dysfunction of your psychology. It has mostly to do with feeling that you are owed or that you have been slighted or offended in some way or you fear that you might be. This term ties together many different kinds of emotional dysfunctions like keeping accounts and complaining and justifying, and many others. Vanity plays a powerful role in Inner Considering as does Fear. The psychological expression of it goes something like this: you arrive late at a

party with a great story about your delay. Everyone is already engaged in conversations and activities. No one seems especially interested in inviting you to join them or in your great story. You feel slighted. You feel that these people aren't treating you very well. They are not showing you the amount of interest, regard and appreciation you deserve. You feel insulted and offended and you begin to worry about what every one of them thinks about you. Do they like you? Do they notice that you are nervous? Can they tell that you exaggerate? Do they agree with what you are saying, approve of it, of you? Of how you look? What if they don't agree with you? Are they criticizing you, scoffing, dismissing, mocking, belittling you? These feelings are based on the unarticulated question in your mind that feels like am I satisfied? ....Are you getting your expectations and requirements of this event fulfilled?

Inner Considering is always saying things like I hope they like me; What if I make a mistake?; What do they think of me?; Was that an insult?; What did he mean by that?; I hope I don't embarrass myself; What if I do something humiliating?; What will they think?; Are they in agreement with me?; Is someone trying to make me look bad?; Why is that person not paying attention?. It moves very quickly into even more general Negative Emotions. Most often they are about how dissatisfied you are with your life and your circumstances and how unfairly treated you feel by them. You feel that you never got a break or that you have had exceptionally bad circumstances. You feel that you should have a better job and higher position and more ease in your life. You feel that life has cheated you out of the opportunity to have what you want. You think you haven't received the proper share of consideration, appreciation, or compensation that you deserve from life and people.

This very complex, wide-ranging psychological Wrong Work is a huge area of study that you undertake in order to be free of it. Every form of Inner Considering is an obstruction to the development of Consciousness. Inner Considering keeps you focused on yourself and filled with your own requirements. This effectively eliminates the possibility of real personal development of transcended consciousness.

27. IDENTIFICATION:

In the Work, being Identified with something means giving the force of your belief to it and ascribing it to yourself. Primarily you are identified with yourself, with who you think you are. Therefore you are identified most with everything that defines you, i.e. your attitudes, your opinions, your politics, religion, national affiliation, cultural designation, as well as individual events and circumstances. This is the mechanical functioning of an unawakened consciousness. In Identification, the psychology goes from one associative thought to another,

Identifying with each one in its turn, giving force to the Identification by believing what it says and asserting it.

You may define yourself as a good citizen, politically liberal, socially acceptable, patriotic, sound minded, honorable person. However you define yourself, it will be expressed in what you believe to be consciously formed attitudes and opinions and dispositions. However, these Identifications are not you and they were not formed Consciously yet they feel like yourself. They are at present who you know yourself to be. But they have been formulated in you without your conscious participation and therefore belong to the level of Sleep. If you can imagine for a moment that you have been struck with total amnesia, thereby you have no attitudes or opinions or preferences or any of the conventional ways to describe yourself, yet you still exist. You are not the things you have lost with your memory.

Identification is one of the most difficult areas to work with, it is the most powerful force keeping us asleep. It is subtle and insidious and powerfully tenacious because it brings you right up to the point of having to forsake your ego for the transcendent higher.

28. MULTIPLICITY:
One of the hallmark transitional points in the Work occurs when you have observed all of the previously

described Wrong Work within yourself and you see the enormity of contradictions and insincerity therein. The Work teaches that your sleeping psychology is an unorganized mass of individual thoughts and feelings called Is. This is the doctrine of Is. To every circumstance in life, an I within you steps forward and says I in response -- without the presence of Real I or Consciousness or intentionality or unity. After a long period of Self-Observation, you notice that many Is are habitual and congregate in groups. You will observe how one I can contradict another I with no seeming discomfort, that you can go to bed full of Is of conviction to wake early in the morning and find only Is of complaint and resistance, justifying and rationalizing away the previous nights Is. You will se that your Is speak automatically for you in ways that you would not choose, were you able to choose. You will see how Is are constantly changing, expressing your mechanical responses to the stimuli in your life. You will understand that in saying I to something you are giving consent and energy to Identification.

One of the reasons this is a critical stage is because in seeing your Multiplicity you have the first glimpse of the magnitude of the Work and the magnitude of its requirements of you. It is a decisive point where you have to commit to the path of unity or decide to live with being a Multiplicity. Thereafter, you will have to make choices about every I you observe within yourself. You will have to work against inconsistency, and you will have to restructure your psychology with no Wrong Work left in it.

More importantly, the mere fact that you know through Verification that you are a Multiplicity means you can choose which Is are real and honest and which express your Real I. Knowing your Multiplicity eventually gives you the power to choose, thereby change.

29. SELF-AWARENESS:

All of the efforts you make to practice Self-Observation, Self-Remembering, not expressing Negative Emotions, and to be Externally Considerate are aimed at bringing you into a higher state of consciousness called Self-Awareness. Practicing Self-Observation over a long period of time and verifying the existence in your own psychology, of the Wrong Work of Inner Considering, lying, justifying, etc., will teach you to know thyself in the only way that matters. Self-Awareness is the beginning point of your potential. Before you reach Self-Awareness, you are too mechanical to be accessible to the influence of higher Understanding, with only rare, brief exceptions throughout your life.

With honest Self-Awareness, you can begin to choose to be real in every moment. It is the point at which real and permanent change in your level of Being can become tangible.

In this System, Self-Awareness, Self-Remembering and Self-Observation all belong to the same level of Consciousness which is directly above your normal consciousness. Each is a different kind of activity. They are not the same thing.

30. INTENTIONALITY:

Intentionality means acting with Conscious awareness. You must reach conscious awareness, even momentarily, in order to act with intentionality. Consciousness and Being manifested in Real I and True Personality act with intentionality.

31. NON-IDENTIFICATION:

Non-Identification is the movement of energy out of Wrong Work. It is the force between mechanicalness and intentionality. In order to be free to choose intentionality, you must be free of your own Identifications, free of your requirements. If you are motivated by selfishness or personal agenda, you are Identified and you are not free to make a pure choice.

Non-Identification is an effort that you make which releases force for transformation. It is that state of selflessness or emptiness or detachment that is referred to in this Work. It happens when you choose not to express or consent to your normal mechanical responses. During the Work process you can experience times of Non-Identification. This state is available to you in every moment when you sacrifice your own requirements in order to act from Conscience, intentionally. It is the state you are seeking in doing the Work.

32. SACRIFICE:

In order to get into a state of Non-Identification, you must sacrifice something. In the Work, you sacrifice everything false or wrong and selfish or negative that belongs to Acquired Personality for self-transcendent consciousness. When you sacrifice your personal requirements and desires, you will find you can reach Non-Identification with the force you have withdrawn from Identification with your own agenda.

Understanding the idea of sacrifice correctly is critical to a straight path. The Work teaches that you must pay for what you receive, and this is correct. What you have to sacrifice in order to Work on yourself is your self-interest, your Acquired Personality with all of its screaming opinions, likes and dislikes, attitudes and hatreds. In doing so you can reach a higher state of consciousness called Non-Identification. It is only from that point that you can formulate right action. So the sacrifice that you must make in order to develop in the Work is a psychological sacrifice of ego to make room for the growth of consciousness and the receptivity to higher influences. Every effort you make to let go of an Identification is a sacrifice. Every effort you make to practice Self-Observation is a sacrifice. Every effort you make to not express Negative Emotions is a sacrifice. These are the sacrifices that are required by any authentic developmental path, in this case the Work. Nothing else can produce any gain in consciousness. You can't buy your way into it and you can't do external work that will get you there. Sacrifice is an essential, emotional/psychological effort. It has force and it leaves space for growth.

33. SUFFERING:
The Work teaches that there are two kinds of suffering -- Necessary Suffering and Unnecessary Suffering. They both feel quite the same and we generally don't differentiate between them. Your suffering over a public humiliation, for instance, may be as severe as your suffering over the loss of a close friend. So it is critical to start observing the difference.

Everyone suffers nearly continuously throughout their lifetime, regardless of their circumstances. And there are valid reasons for Real Suffering in everyone's lifetime. However, the Work teaches us that the vast majority of our suffering is unnecessary. Unnecessary Suffering arises from unsatisfied requirements and desires on our part.

Real Suffering is bearing the loss of love, the death of someone close, meaninglessness, real heart deprivation, illness, etc.

Unnecessary Suffering is what you study most in the Work because it is what you have to sacrifice. Your Unnecessary Suffering arises from your Acquired Personality and its Wrong Work. All forms of Inner Considering are Unnecessary Suffering. All forms of Negative Emotions are Unnecessary Suffering. All forms of justifying, fear, worry, and insecurity are Unnecessary Suffering. The sources of all Wrong Work are addressed in doing the Work, and are gradually eliminated.

There is one more element that needs to be mentioned here. Doing the Work is taking on intentionally additional Necessary Suffering with the aim of development. Doing the Work practices and exercises causes Necessary Suffering and it needs to be done willingly. Accepting the process is Necessary Suffering and sacrificing your egocentric psychology for self-transcendent psychology is Necessary Suffering. You do this for a purpose when you are in the Work.

34. INNER SEPARATION:
Among the practices and exercises in the Work, we are given tools as well to use against any Wrong Work that we observe. These are psychological tools applicable to your psychological development.

First the Work asks you to practice Self-Observation. You are instructed to observe the Multiplicity of Is, the degree of Wrong Work in your psychological condition, and watch passively as you begin to know yourself in a new way. But what then? Once you have seen your Acquired Personality and have sensed your Real I, how do you reconcile them? What can you do about the Wrong Work that you observe within yourself?

The Work gives us a practice called Inner Separation that is a psychological effort you make to step back from your mechanical functioning and view it as only mechanical functioning. In doing so, you strengthen the observer of the mechanics -- Observing I. The effort to distance yourself from mechanical behavior weakens its force. This is a subtle psychological exercise. You see repeated mechanical behavior and you do not say I to it. You do not assent. Your rob it of force. It moves away from you. It amounts to reaching for detachment or taking one step in the direction of Non-Identification. Every effort of this nature helps to separate you from your False Personality.

35. INNER STOP:

Another valuable tool that the Work gives us is called Inner Stop. It can be considered the first movement of effort toward Inner Separation and Non-Identification. When you observe Wrong Work in yourself and you know through Verification that this is Wrong Work that you wish to change and that the first effort of change is to stop the Wrong Work, you can practice Inner Stop. If you observe yourself justifying, simply stop saying the words. If you can successfully stop some Wrong Work in process, then you have the choice in that moment to move toward separation from that Wrong Work. Elimination of it happens by not consenting to giving it your attention. First you stop, then you can move toward Inner Separation. You can use methods of remembrance of the Work and your aim or some other intentional activity to assist you in changing direction at that point.

36. INNER SILENCE:
In the Work, Inner Silence is a very specific psychological exercise. It is not the inner silence commonly referred to when speaking of a transcendent state above the noise of the Multiplicity. It is not the general inner silence of a still, inactive mind. It means to remain silent in your mind toward one specific thing.

As you practice Self-Observation, you will begin to see definite, repetitive groups of Is that are harmful or dishonest or even dangerous. You will observe yourself singing your song. You will observe an account you are keeping against someone. When you have a definite set of Is that you have recognized repeatedly over a period of time through Self-Observation, you can practice the

Works version of Inner Silence in relation to these familiar sets of Is in order to disempower them. The practice of Inner Silence goes something like this. You are aware that there is an account raging in your head against another person. Fueled by Negative Emotions, it has its own momentum. Its energy is actively present as are the consequent Negative Emotions. To practice Inner Silence, stop giving voice to that particular set of Is. Every time an I arises that belongs to keeping an account against that person, you give it no words either literally or more specifically psychologically. You do not let your thoughts touch that place in your psychology and you do not let your tongue touch that place because if it does the words will pour forth. So in practicing Inner Silence, first, you give no words to the specific Wrong Work. You give it no attention, even if you still sense its presence. You refuse to acknowledge or have your attention drawn into it. But most importantly, you do not allow yourself to speak the words even in your mind.

37. EXTERNAL CONSIDERING:
If you persevere in the Work and develop on its path, and when you have reached some degree of self-transcendence, you will begin to be able to practice External Considering intentionally. The Work asks you to practice External Considering from the very beginning of your efforts. At first, this seems mostly an issue of exag-

gerated good manners, but as you go through the process of the Work, your Understanding of what it means and what it takes to be externally considerate in the full sense is beyond your capacity for a very long time.

To be externally considerate, very well includes sensitive manners. But it asks you not only to be polite, it asks you to understand the other persons position. It asks that you view the circumstances from the others point of view and that you treat the other person with intentionality that expresses good will -- Conscious Love. It may require being active or it may require being passive, or even withdrawing. Every day, every bit of time you spend in the company of others becomes an opportunity to practice self-transcendence through External Considering. As you do this exercise and develop in the Work, you begin to have an organic Understanding of what it means to be asleep. And as you begin to awaken yourself, you will find it becomes very easy to forgive other people for their condition because you know what being asleep is like. It is full of suffering.

External Considering requires a good deal of practice and study that will be useful to you when you gain enough consciousness to choose self-transcendence. But the essential nature and foundation of External Considering is based in forgiveness. It is forgiving people for being asleep. In doing this, you release them from your requirements and you both become free. It means giving others ease and whatever consideration needed. Acting intentionally from Conscience with Understanding and right actions -- to do what is Good.

LECTURE 4

Before you begin practicing the psychological Work of the Fourth Way, you must first have a strong desire to change the kind of human being you are; a reaching out metaphysically, seeking meaning and authenticity and growth into what you were born to become. This kind of dissatisfaction with yourself as you are is a prerequisite because the Work can then use the energy of that desire to fuel the real change it is aimed at. Since the Work is a path devoted to concrete change so must the student be seeking actual change. Each student must be willing to undertake the efforts necessary due to a sincere longing for personal development.

The Work must be done willingly and this is a most critical point. First, you must understand what you are doing and why you are doing it before you can do it willingly. If you try to engage in the Work practices in an uninformed or casual way, or out of curiosity, or if you are simply following the directions given you by your Teacher, in a legalistic manner, you will find that you have bitten off more than you can chew and the Work will become hazardous to you. Again, if you are generally satisfied with yourself the Work will only offend you. Or if you imagine that you can gain the kind of self-mastery which will give you the power to fulfill your dreams and desires and thus be satisfied, you will be in for a rude shock. None of these approaches will get you anywhere in the Work. From the outset, you must willingly be seeking sincere self-change in order for the Work to work in you. If you understand this clearly and you have the right attitude, which is Conscience toward the Work, then you begin with acquiring knowledge.

Gaining knowledge is the first effort in the Work because you cannot get the right results until you understand how and why and what you must do. Since the Work is esoteric knowledge it is of a special quality which requires thinking. You cannot learn about the ideas and exercises intellectually, by rote using your ordinary memory, and get any results. The ideas of this system need to be assimilated into your consciousness by way of understanding which is not the same thing as knowing. This requires personal Work, thought and reflection and a flexible mind which doesn't presume it understands everything already.

You can spend your lifetime studying the knowledge of the Fourth Way, becoming a technical expert, and never actually be in the path of the Work. Knowledge comes first but it goes nowhere until you apply it to yourself, to your Being. No amount of knowledge alone creates change, but when you begin to practice what you have learned you receive light and gradually the ideas become organic understanding by way of the personal experience you have in practicing them.

Studying this esoteric teaching will give you small shocks of awakening if you reflect on the ideas. The idea that humanity is asleep is a shock only slightly less alarming than the idea that you are asleep. The idea of self-evolution and different levels of consciousness is a shock. And the idea of Multiplicity and mechanicalness can leave you reeling. You can find momentary mind expansion but not permanent personal transformation in the knowledge of this teaching. Transformation, which clearly indicates change, happens in and through your individual effort to apply this knowledge to yourself by way of practicing its teaching. Too many students confuse knowing about the ideas of the System with understanding that only comes with the enlightenment gained in practical efforts. You may know that you do not remember yourself, but that knowing doesn't mean you are remembering yourself. You have to make the efforts to actually remember yourself in order to understand what it means that you don't remember yourself. You may know quite well that you must observe yourself but never get beyond merely noticing this or that randomly, or you may have a very clear grasp of the idea of mechanicalness without ever having observed your own. You cannot have the perspective of the Third State of Consciousness unless you reach up into it in a practical way through your effort.

Getting into the Third State of Consciousness -- awakening -- is made possible mostly by way of making your personality passive; by going against the mechanical momentum of sleep which is always asserting your personality. Remember that the Third State is available to you at all times, above your ordinary state, accessible by the means of practicing Self-Remembering and Self-Observation and Non-Identification which are conditions of consciousness in the Third State. You can create these conditions yourself by doing the Work yourself. That is what self-evolution means.

This is an incredible idea -- that you can raise yourself up into higher levels of Being and Consciousness within yourself by doing the Work, and in doing so, you can receive enlightenment. The magnitude of this gift of opportunity exceeds words, yet it is verifiable and true. Your valuation of the Work will deepen and grow as you learn to appreciate the significance of this gift. If you find this esoteric path, you may consider yourself blessed.

THE PRACTICE OF SELF-REMEMBERING

Every student beginning to practice the psychological exercises of the Work is taught first of all to practice Self-Remembering in a particular form. You are instructed to call to attention your remembrance of your most authentic Self; recollecting the essential sense of your Being, outside of time and events. Several times a day, or whenever you remember to, practice Self-Remembering by standing upright within yourself outside of the moment and its influences. It makes no difference whether you follow an alarm clock method of practicing Self-Remembering or if you simply try to remember to remember yourself. What you will discover first is that indeed you do not remember yourself. You will start remembering that you forget yourself and this is the beginning of light.

Since this exercise relies on something more pure in motivation than rules, legalism rarely works well. Keeping a notebook of your experiences may be helpful if it is your style, or it may disrupt the experience or your perception of it if it is not your style. What is important is that you actually practice Self-Remembering and that you taste that state and remember it.

All of the other psychological Work practices are different forms and degrees of Self-Remembering. Self-Observation is not Self-Remembering although it allows you to observe that you do not remember yourself. This is where the confusion lies between Self-Observation and Self-Remembering. Self-Remembering and Self-Observation are very different kinds of psychological activities that touch the same state of consciousness, the Third State. Self-Awareness and Real I belong to this level as well, each resonating to some degree in the others, or sharing the same taste of state.

The Work teaches that bringing the Work ideas to the moment of experience (incoming impressions) is also a form of Self-Remembering. Practicing any Work exercise, i.e. Self-Observation, Inner Separation, etc. is a form of Self-Remembering. Remembering your Aim is another form. In full Self-Remembering, it is your Real I that is experienced in relation to all things; your individuality, your nothingness, your interwoven place in the universe. In this state you feel profound peace and inexpressible enlightenment. It cannot be reduced to adequate words. Although everyone has had moments of this experience during their lifetime, the practicing of Self-Remembering can intentionally evoke this state and help to develop it into a permanent condition of Consciousness. This kind of permanence must be built upon practice. You must Remember Yourself -- no one else can do this for you.

SELF-OBSERVATION

Watch, do not sleep.

Self-Observation is the most fundamental practice in this Teaching. Even more so than Self-Remembering because it provides the light of Consciousness and the means for developing your Real I -- the one meant to be remembered in the act of full Self-Remembering. Everything begins with and depends upon Self-Observation in the Work. The subsequent practices and exercises all depend upon it and Real I is illuminated by it. It is consequently critical that your practice of Self-Observation is refined and accurate. For this you will need a Teacher.

When you begin to practice Self-Observation, you must divide yourself into two sides, an observed side and an observing side. To do so, you must take part of your attention and create a vantage point within your psychology from which you can see yourself objectively. When you try to see yourself from this new position, you should be able to see all at once -- your outer circumstances, your actions and words, your attitudes, emotional states, posture, tone of voice and inflection, intentions, motives, facial expressions, and body movements. This kind of awareness takes some practice and only comes in small glimpses at first. Each glimpse is a photograph of yourself that you will remember because of the special quality it has. And each effort to practice Self-Observation will create more light because Self-Observation lets a ray of light from Higher Consciousness into your psychology.

The analogy for practicing Self-Observation goes like this. You have many Is, one of which is Observing I, and you are attending a play. The play represents life. The audience, your many different Is, are each giving their attention to the play and each responding differently to it. Some Is are excited, some are bored, some are angry, some are pleased. Observing I turns around from the stage and watches the audience, noticing each Is reaction to the play which is life.

Remembering to practice Self-Observation and refining that practice are the first two challenges.
Reminding yourself can be a simple matter of taping up notes that say Observe yourself all over your environment, or deciding to practice at a particular time every day, or using small tricks which remind you to observe yourself.

Once you begin to practice Self-Observation, you will be horrified at times regarding what you observe. This is the biggest obstacle to overcome in the refining of your practice of Self-Observation. When you observe yourself and you begin to see the insincerity, the lies and selfishness and the legion of Negative Emotions that characterize your inner experience and shape your life, the shock can stop you in your tracks, in a literal way, developmentally speaking. As soon as you feel Negative Emotions about what you are observing, like guilt, fear, humiliation, frustration or shame, you are immediately stuck. Since nothing conscious can grow from a negative state, you are effectively stopped. As soon as you begin justifying what you have observed, you are equally stopped. If your are justifying, you may be sure that you are identified and in Negative Emotions.

It is vital to practice Self-Observation uncritically. You must be able to see everything clearly with a dispassionate eye. This does not mean that you become oblivious to Conscience, but you must learn not to ascribe everything to yourself. Doing so is Identification which is the condition you are seeking to change. The process of the Work will enlighten you about what to ascribe to yourself -- your Real I.

The first thing to do in the case of becoming negative in response to what you observe in yourself, is to withdraw the feeling of I from it. Say to this observation: This is not I. Then turn your Observing I on your negative responses and notice what they say to you. When you say This is not I you are differentiating between your mechanics and your Real I, which is clarifying, and you are making a small withdrawal of force from the energy of mechanicalness. If you find yourself justifying, simply stop saying the words. Practice Inner Silence.

It will take a long time of actual practice before Observing I functions accurately or has any permanence, or before you have experienced enough internal light to verify what the Work teaches regarding your own psychology.

The light of Self-Observation shines a ray into the darkness that is the unconscious side of you. This darkness is not evil. You are not instructed to look for whatever evil might be unacknowledged in you. That idea of confronting inner darkness is evil. Your dark side very well contains multitudes of Negative Emotions, but that is not all. Your dark side is all that remains unobserved and unacknowledged by you, unconscious to you. You cannot change something if you have no awareness of its existence. So real personal change, which is the aim of esotericism, depends upon the light of Self-Observation first of all.

Some of the many reasons the Work asks you to observe your Negative Emotions and states from the beginning are because they are not part of your Essence, they are acquired and most importantly they stand squarely in the way of your development. Also, each student in the Work is asked to not give expression to negativity from the beginning, as work on Being. In doing so, you will begin to see the stranglehold Negative Emotions have on you and you will feel their force when you try not to express them. But first, you must be able to observe them.

Your practice will show you how you go from complaining to feeling irritable to speaking and acting with anger followed by self-justification, feeling dejected and guilty. You will observe inner and outer talking in slanderous terms and find yourself grumbling about something you must endure, worrying about it. You will see how you are constantly being critical about everyone and everything you encounter. And this is what you call discernment. You will notice that you are plagued with dissatisfaction no matter what you have and you feel anxious and fearfully vulnerable. When things are going well, you will be afraid that they will change and you will suffer. When things are not going well, you will be afraid that they wont change and you will suffer. In any case, you are afraid and already suffering. You will catch yourself reciting grudges against people and events and circumstances and you will observe frustration. You will catch yourself gossiping, be shocked by how often you lie, feel insecure, embarrassed or rejected, or how often you flatter yourself, judge others, and relate to everything in terms of like and dislike.

It is very clear that all of this Wrong Work in your psychology must be eliminated before you can function at a higher level of consciousness. Self-Observation is the first step in beginning to purify your inner life; in getting rid of all of the mess and uncleanliness of Negative Emotions. When you observe a negative I, you are already less under its power. Observing I is not identified and so cannot be captivated. It uses the force of intentionality which would otherwise be engaged in the mechanical negative emotion. Repeatedly observing the same Negative Emotions weakens them and makes separation from them progressively easier.

Students are also asked to observe their False Personality in action. This includes: attitudes, opinions, preferences, mannerisms, repetitive phrases, postures, body language, facial expressions and the whole multitude of changing Is. This stimulus-response multitude is called Imaginary I and it has the illusion of unity. The formulation of it comes from ideas you have about who you are. These illusory ideas form pictures of yourself based on imagination, vanity, and self-love. Imaginary I believes that it is the pictures and imagination you have about yourself, but honest Self-Observation will show you that you are not as you suppose yourself to be. All of the multitude of Is spring from automatic responses which are dictated by your individual Acquired Personality. Self-Observation will show you that you are not your False Personality.

After you have practiced Self-Observation for a time, when you have a Work memory full of photographs of yourself and verifications, the idea of Multiplicity will begin to have more meaning to you. Seeing that you have no stable center or controlling I means that you are not living life -- you are only responding to stimuli. That is a very grave bit of understanding which, if you get hold of it, will increase your desire for change.

This point in the Work can be frighteningly disorienting. Becoming aware of your Multiplicity happens in the

Work process long before your Real I or True Personality have the strength of presence to save you from the psychological vertigo of feeling your nothingness in the acute manner that Self-Observation creates. It is here that the first really dangerous place in the Work is reached. When you get a first harsh look at all of the hordes of Is in your psychology over which you have no control, and you see them reacting mechanically to life without your assent and when you hear them say things that you don't mean, you suddenly feel like a stranger to yourself. You don't recognize the mass of changing Is as a reflection of how you have always pictured yourself and so the illusion of unity and Imaginary I is dissolved.

What follows is the question: Who am I? This is the necessary condition that must be reached -- in the moment of reality when you are experiencing your true nothingness, to feel the question Who am I? If your motives are sincere, the response you receive is an assertion of your Real I.

You begin to perceive your Observing I as separate from the other Is in quality and position. It stands apart, above the other Is so to speak, and can see them in action. Remember that Observing I informs and defines Real I and Real I stands above Observing I. This perception becomes a tangible inner experience as you proceed in the process through Self-Observation. You begin to feel your sense of self as different from the Is of False Personality. The difference becomes space between False Personality and Real I defining both. But this process takes time and Observing I has the ability to see before it gains the strength to act. You will feel the falsehood of the Is of Personality and know that this is not I, yet be unable to change anything. What is worse, you wont know what is I having no developed sense of your Real I yet.

It takes a level of stable, mature Being and accurate instruction to traverse this part of the path. It can be valuable at this point to ask yourself this question: What is it within me that is doing the observing?. The answer gives Observing I clarity and definition. The more often you practice Self-Observation the more quickly you can pass through this stage in the Work as Observing I becomes more defined.

In practicing Self-Observation, Observing I will see the Multiplicity of Is, habitual Personality traits, Negative Emotions, associative thinking, self-justifying, Inner Considering, fear and vanity each vying for your attention and using your energy. At such a moment of seeing a discerning choice has to be made, one that negates all Is that are false or negative and also attracts and affirms all Is that belong to Higher Consciousness within you. The faculty that can make this kind of discernment is Real Conscience which becomes active in the light of Self-Observation.

Right here, at this point in the process of the Work, is where the purity of your motives comes into play. If your Work is serious, and your Aim is Gods Will and not your own, then Real Conscience will discern and choose and inspire you. Otherwise the opportunity is lost when an I of Personality imagines that it chooses, selecting what pleases it most. In this case, False Personality is strengthened and nothing is gained in terms of the Work.

It is only in the purity and humility of your nothingness that Objective Real Conscience can illuminate the Real I of your Being. So if you have been Working from a false basis such as a desire for gaining personal power, this is the point at which you will fail due to your motives. It is a tragedy perpetuated by corrupt schools and corrupt teachers teaching corrupt motives and professing corrupt aims.

The Work takes the place of Real Conscience while your own emerges. Conscience is a function of spirit that needs a degree of purity in order to become active. Self-serving, self-aggrandizing motives haven't the purity to accommodate the activity of Conscience. And if you find yourself at this point of choosing in the Work process without the assistance of Real Conscience in discernment and choice, you have no connection with higher Mind to guide you. This is a very dangerous psychological position in which to find yourself. Having no direction, you cannot move out of the stage of seeing your Multiplicity toward unity and authenticity, and you cannot un-know what you have seen and verified. Such misguided motivation leads students directly to the point of soul-shattering loss of identity and it leaves them there, when the real aim of the Work is creating unity and authentic I.

However, let us suppose that your motives are right and you do come to the point in the Work when you have to choose which Is to nurture and which to eliminate. To speak in very practical terms, suppose you observe yourself justifying being critical of someone.

Well, he is very bad you know. He is rude and stupid and he's caused you great difficulty, even pain. He talks too much and finds sarcasm amusing, not caring if he causes offense. He even deliberately insulted you and tried to undermine you with callous disregard for your feelings. You've heard him lie and gossip and slander everyone he talks about. And his clothes and that hair! You'd think that someone so intent on making a spectacle of themselves would care more about their appearance. You suspect he has a problem with drugs or alcohol and are almost sure that he steals and cheats others. You really can't stand him and with good reason.

Now if you observe some thoughts and feelings like this going on in yourself and you remember the Work ideas and your aim, you will have to think about them in relation to this event. First, you STOP criticizing because it is a negative emotion and the Work teaches you that to stop expressing Negative Emotions is central to the process. Then you have to practice STOP again and again as the thoughts and feelings return repeatedly, resisting your aim. Then you recognize that your personal mechanics are at work since someone else finds this fellow quite charming and witty, even loveable -- maybe his mother -- and others take no note of him at all. So it is your subjective mechanical responses to him which are at fault. Your Negative Emotions are always your own fault. But how can you possibly not object to him and his behavior?

Then you remember that he is also subject to his mechanicalness and dead to the world Asleep in it. It dawns on you that he is not his behavior anymore than you are your behavior. Having observed your own inability to behave always intentionally, you understand what being mechanical means and that he has very little choice in the matter. You realize that his mean-spirited personality had to have been formed by pain and imitation and that his constant snide remarks are an attempt to make others seem less than himself so that he can feel superior. You know then that he actually feels very inferior and insecure and that his personality is driven by these conditions. A moment of compassion enters you through understanding. You think am I so different? You see that your criticism and slanderous thoughts of him aren't very different from his gossiping, slandering, insulting behavior. You verify that suspicion accommodates the facts to suit your negative attitude while you are sitting in your own superior little nitch looking down on him, judging and condemning him for looking down on others. Is your feeling of superiority any more correct than his? Have you ever acted badly in order to get attention or power? Can you remember the last time you lied or gossiped or said an unkind word about someone -- today? It doesn't matter if your expression of these things is not like his. You see that they are the same Negative Emotions in action in him and in yourself. You understand insecurity and the pain of feeling inferior very well from personal experience and long-term Self-Observation. You experience an affinity with him. You realize that you do not know the real person, you see only the False Personality which is actually more painful to him than to you. You feel remorse for being so critical and mean-spirited toward him. You are humbled and you feel the pain that you inflicted within yourself. You desire forgiveness and you need purity. You recognize that you have been given the immeasurable gift of the Work and its ability to free you from Negative Emotions and the suffering they create. Then you remember that this person has not received that opportunity and you feel sympathy and compassion for him. A prayer arises in your heart that he be also blessed. You feel forgiven and your are freed. This more purified and enlightened state is an experience of your Real I. Its consistent presence is built upon repetitive experience.

It is not necessary that you learn to like everything you consider bad or negative. And here is another point in esoteric teaching which gets misinterpreted regularly. The idea of learning to like what you dislike is an exercise meant to be practiced with discernment and an appropriate spiritual disposition of releasing your subjective requirements. If a man spits in the street in front of you, you do not have to like it. However, you must forgive him knowing that he is unconscious in his imitated mechanics. He does not know what he is doing, he is asleep. And so you can forgive him since he is already suffering the pangs of Sleep -- a condition you are very familiar with.

Often this part of transformation teaching gets distorted into the practice of accepting everything passively, without Conscience active which will lead only to confusion. Sometimes, as in monasticism and misguided Fourth Way groups, this idea becomes the practice of creating more suffering or friction in order to generate more transformation. This approach does not work because creating suffering means missing the mark in this system. You can be assured that your everyday life is full of all the suffering and artifice you can handle to fuel your Work for your lifetime.

This is an example of one of the infinite possible experiences of transformation created in doing the Work. It leaves you feeling purified, clearer, lighter with a new perspective and tolerance and broader view with connected understanding. If you undertake these practices correctly and you persevere in them, you will find that you must struggle with many issues, and the same ones repeatedly. You will also find liberated authenticity.

Notice how much choosing has to do with this process. To begin with, you choose to practice Self-Observation intentionally, you choose to give it your attention and effort. This is what is meant by doing the Work willingly. You choose to stop your mechanics and consider your internal responses objectively in the light of the Work ideas. You choose to accept what you see and take responsibility for it. You choose to remember your aim. You choose to allow yourself to be humbled and transformed. You choose with integrity the thoughts you think, the words you use, the emotions you consent to. You choose your actions and motives, you choose to forgive and externally consider, you choose which influences to which you submit yourself.

It is just incredibly intelligent that something in you higher than your vacillating personality makes these choices. Real Conscience needs to be that which chooses. Real Conscience becomes active when you choose to make Personality passive and follow the Work. All of these profound things depend upon Self-Observation. In the Work, transformation depends upon Self-Observation above all.

This process, which amounts to intentionally pulling yourself up into a higher state of consciousness, must be put into practice an incalculable number of times in order to build a new psychological structure from which you have the perspective of developed understanding.

A simple overview of the process would work something like this if you were practicing all of the Work correctly: you observe something about yourself, your Acquired Personality, or some negative emotion which you feel and know must be changed. From the vantage point of solid Self-Observation you have a foothold from which to say This is not I and feel the separation between Observing I and personality I. The defining of this distance between Observing I and Acquired Personality helps to accomplish Inner Separation.

After you have observed a specific thing and identified it and you are intentionally working against it, you will have to practice Inner Separation and Inner Silence, Directed Attention, inner and outer Stop, Non-Identification, and bring all of the ideas of the Work to bear on the problem. As you observe the issue repeatedly and refuse to identify with it repeatedly, it moves farther and farther away from you over time until it becomes faint. It loses strength and sounds hollow and false. You will see what Wrong Work it is connected to in your psyche and consequently be increasingly able to say This is not I to it. Eventually the issue you are working on will be dissolved in the light of

Understanding and transcended. Usually it takes a long time for Self-Observation to produce these results. But sometimes an issue you have to deal with will simply vanish as soon as you see it objectively. The results are the same in each case. You are free and more conscious -- Non-Identified.

NON-IDENTIFICATION

The psychological state called Non-Identified in the Work is a condition of detachment, not from life, but from the power and influences life has over you. There is a very subtle difference. It does not mean not caring about life in an unemotional dismissal of its significance. It means transcending your subjective responses to and requirements of life in favor of higher, more conscious emotions. It takes effort to achieve the self-transcendence of Non-Identification but if you reach that state, the state itself feels effortless. It is lighter because it is not attached to the heavy coarser energy of Negative Emotions. It feels clearer because from a higher perspective of consciousness you can see more, you can see connections, scale and relativity, and this gives you understanding which brings freedom and peace.

The true form of this state must be reached through developed Understanding. Understanding has force, it can build Consciousness and create Non-Identification. You can sometimes jump into detachment temporarily without the understanding that accompanies developing a more permanent condition of Non-Identification, but be careful not to use this practice for emotionally dissociative escapism. That distortion of practice cannot build anything. It means missing the mark of the aim of the practice.

Real Non-Identification is a conscious activity even though a good deal of the effort is in making personality passive. Personality is always concerned first with what it thinks it wants. You have to get to the point of not forever wanting what you think you want so that you can will the Work and want what it teaches instead. Making your own will passive in this way is a very intentional conscious activity. It requires energy and attention and it is not a matter of passively abdicating responsibility or Conscience. The ultimate and achievable result is wanting only Gods Will, which is the nature of the state of Non-Identification.

TEACHERS AND SCHOOLS

The Work is a very clean, pure path where sincerity, honesty, and integrity are essential and the right aim is pursued from the beginning. The intellectual ideas of the Work become emotional understanding through your personal practice. It is surely very clear that you must learn from someone who understands this path. You cannot get the right instruction in the Work from someone who merely knows about it. Many people know the Fourth Way ideas thoroughly but do not possess the developed understanding necessary to teach them from the right angle. Having a bad teacher in the Work, whether an unscrupulous fraud or simply one who has no understanding, is a seriously dangerous situation that can damage, even cripple your psychology simply because it isn't taught with Conscience or Understanding and the true Aim.

Although the System contains vast intellectual ideas that you can study and ponder for yourself, the transformational personal inner Work absolutely requires one to one, face to face, work with a Teacher. An advanced student can teach the cosmology and basic practices under the direction of a teacher. But addressing your individual experiences, adjusting your practices, guiding you through the process -- these things have to come from someone who has gained a degree of developed Understanding by way of personal experience.

An authentic Teacher in the Fourth Way Work teaches from love to preserve the Teaching and to give it to others and to continue their own personal growth. A real Teacher need not be a divine being or even a perfect one, but there are a few recognizable, verifiable requirements for the position. A Teacher in the Work needs to have personal integrity and a high standard of Conscience. You should be able to see exemplary behavior and Being. What your Teacher says to you should lead you into Understanding. The instructions you receive should also lead you deeper into Understanding. You should be able to verify the results of employing your Teachers instructions and feel a new quality of Being growing.

This is perhaps where the greatest difficulty lies. No qualified teachers have been produced from the major groups descending from Gurdjieff, Ouspensky, and Nicoll because this Teaching has been so distorted and removed from its aim and context by today's generation of teachers and schools. Numerous groups exist, from small conversational or study groups to international schools and organizations claiming thousands of members. But no real teachers. That means no real schools.

Without question, the best possible circumstance in which to meet and practice the Work is, or would be, an authentic school. If you are taking this path seriously, it is very beneficial to have relationship with other serious students. You can learn from each others experiences and compound your knowledge and understanding through discussion, and you can verify for each other the quality of your teacher. There are no currently known schools or teachers in this sense. In fact, there are many unscrupulous pseudo teachers and fraudulent groups using the Fourth Way, or rather misusing it, for their own gain without concern for any harm they cause.

Anyone interested in pursuing the Fourth Way needs to be very careful today when searching out a school. Be well read in the Gurdjieff, Ouspensky and Nicoll writings on the Fourth Way, particularly the Psychological Commentaries by Nicoll. Ask lots of questions. Be willing to submit yourself to the Work and to respect and value your Teacher without letting go of the bit of Real Conscience you have alive in Magnetic Center -- the bit that knows that Goodness is above Truth. Remember that the nature of the Absolute is Perfect Goodness and so do not submit yourself to anything that is not goodness. Do not let yourself be convinced that you will lose the Work if you leave any particular group. The Work does not belong to the school. Your real personal Work belongs to you and you can practice it -- be in the Work -- anytime, anywhere. The Work is designed so that you can develop a permanent faculty of perception which is your own Inner Teacher. This is called the indwelling of the Holy Spirit.

www.ingramcontent.com/pod-product-compliance
Lightning Source LLC
Chambersburg PA
CBHW071126090426
42736CB00012B/2030

Acknowledgements

I would like to acknowledge all the personal sacrifices that my family has made over the past 18 years. My husband Terry Sweat has been the backbone of my life and my encourager through the hard times of ministry. My children and grandchildren have loved me and continue to love me when I have been called away to help a woman in need.

I am grateful to Janice Brewton for her dedication to this project. To the members of the Board of Bethesda House of Mercy, past and present, I say thank you for standing with me to accomplish this assignment.

Most of all I wish to thank Jesus for giving me an opportunity to serve Him. The material you are about to read is revelation, revealed through experience and study by the Holy Spirit. I wish to thank Jesus for revealing these truths to me.

Dedication

This work is dedicated to the members of the body of Christ who are looking for a way out of life's toughest issues. These issues have found their place in our churches and in our Christian homes. This work is dedicated to healing and restoration of those who suffer with and from these hard issues of life.